THE STRENGTH
OF THE WEAK

THE STRENGTH
OF THE WEAK
Toward a Christian
Feminist Identity

by DOROTHEE SOELLE

Translated by ROBERT and RITA KIMBER

THE WESTMINSTER PRESS
Philadelphia

Chapters 1–7 and 11–15 are taken from *Sympathie* by Dorothee Soelle (Stuttgart: Kreuz Verlag, 1978); Chapter 16 is from *Das Recht ein anderer zu werden* by Dorothee Soelle (Stuttgart: Kreuz Verlag, 1979); translation by Robert and Rita Kimber.

Chapter 9 appeared originally in Concilium 17 (1981) as "Vater, Macht und Barbarei" and is reprinted here with permission of T. & T. Clark, Ltd., Edinburgh; translation by T. L. Westow.

Scripture quotations from the Revised Standard Version of the Bible are copyrighted 1946, 1952, © 1971, 1973 by the Division of Christian Education of the National Council of the Churches of Christ in the U.S.A. and are used by permission.

"What Am I?" by Clorox (Frank Cleveland) is reprinted from *The Me Nobody Knows*, edited by Stephen Joseph. Copyright © 1969 by Stephen Joseph. Reprinted by permission of Avon Books, New York.

"Who Am I?" by Dietrich Bonhoeffer, from his *Letters and Papers from Prison*, edited by Eberhard Bethge, revised, enlarged edition, published by SCM Press, London, 1971, Copyright © 1953, 1967, 1971 by SCM Press, Ltd., is reprinted by permission of SCM Press and Macmillan Publishing Company, New York.

BOOK DESIGN BY ALICE DERR

Published by The Westminster Press®
Philadelphia, Pennsylvania

PRINTED IN THE UNITED STATES OF AMERICA
9 8 7 6 5 4 3 2 1

Library of Congress Cataloging in Publication Data

Soelle, Dorothee.
  The strength of the weak.

  Bibliography: p.
  1. Feminism—Religious aspects—Christianity.
2. Woman (Christian theology) I. Title.
HQ1154.S58 1984   305.4'2   83-27348
ISBN 0-664-24623-0 (pbk.)

Contents

II. FOUNDATIONS OF A FEMINIST THEOLOGY

Publisher's Note

Over the years, Dorothee Soelle has challenged both European and American readers with insightful writing on a great variety of social, ethical, literary, and theological topics. The thoughts collected here in English for the first time show as never before the depth and scope of her reflections on feminist identity, particularly as these illuminate its relationship to Christian faith and to human liberation. Though gathered from several sources and created originally for quite divers contexts, these writings embody the drive to radicalization and the passionate involvement that have always been the hallmark of her work. It should not be forgotten that the first dedication of much of what is brought to publication in English here was to Elisabeth Käsemann, born on May 11, 1947, who died a victim of dictatorship in Buenos Aires on May 24, 1977.

I
FAITH
AND SOCIETY

1
REBELLION
AGAINST BANALITY
On the Problem of Religion

Meaning and credibility have become scarce. The demand exceeds the supply. We all talk not only about an economic and technological crisis but also about an ideological crisis, a lack of meaning in our private lives, a lack of credibility in public life. If we listen carefully, we realize that all this discussion focuses on the oldest of human questions, the religious questions, couched, however, in an idiom that avoids explicitly religious language as assiduously as our grandparents avoided explicit references to sex.

What does it mean to experience significance in life, to feel certain that life has significance? And what does it mean to derive from our faith in this significance certain values that demand our lasting allegiance, values like the dignity of human life, justice, freedom? What—to use the technocratic term—is this "religious verification of meaning" that most people are lacking but that most seem to want? Why is theology currently reinvestigating the nature of religion even though dialectical theology earlier in our century supposedly disposed of religion once and for all, condemning it as a mere human construct inimical to faith?

In these reflections on the role of religion I will use two persons of my acquaintance as points of reference. Both are German women in their early sixties. Their background is rural lower class, and the key experiences of their lives were those of World War II and the postwar years.

Mrs. K has been a widow for five years. At the end of the war she fled from Pomerania to Hamburg. Since her husband's death she has been renting two rooms in her apartment to supplement her pension. Her contact with her tenants and with other people in her apartment building is about the only human contact she still has. She did not want to have children, she says.

Her life consists of taking care of her apartment, going shopping—a chore she sometimes does for her tenants—and cooking for herself alone. In the afternoons she often watches television. Her reading is limited to an occasional illustrated magazine. It is not easy to maintain a conversation with her, even though she is a voluble talker. She repeats herself and tells the same jokes over and over again. She is most animated when the conversation turns to "the good old days": to Pomerania, work service, and rural life. But even in these areas her memories are limited and never go beyond her own experience. She knows nothing about her grandparents. Her vocabulary is minimal.

Mrs. S lives in the same small town where she was born. Her husband was killed in the war, and she has visited his grave regularly over the last thirty years. She raised five children, three of whom still live in her village and visit her every Sunday after church. She lives with one of her daughters, and her morning routine probably differs very little from that of Mrs. K: shopping, cleaning, cooking, mending. In the afternoon, Mrs. S often retires to her own room for a while, either to read in her prayerbook or simply to sit, toward dusk, with folded hands.

Religion is part of her life and is not subject to question. She goes to Mass on Sundays and sees to it that her grandchildren go too. When, not long ago, a rebellious granddaughter refused to go "there" anymore, it was Mrs. S who had a heart-to-heart talk with the wayward one, a talk that consisted not of arguments but of complaints that Mrs. S repeated until finally obliged to give up. Religion plays a major part in Mrs. S's social life, too. She reads her church's newsletter and complains about the priest. Both these activities help integrate her into the life of the village.

Mrs. K in Hamburg lives without religion. She, like many others, was superficially christianized by instruction for confirmation, but her religion had no meaning either socially or individually. When Mrs. K fled her home village, she easily shed whatever snippets of religion still clung to her. Religion has had no influence on her as a person. It has never meant anything to her. Her system of values seems, in some strange way, neutralized.

She once observed, "Work is all we've got." (Such a remark clearly springs from a despair so deep that it cannot find expression in any medium.) Her relations with her neighbors are limited to competitiveness in what she consumes and in adherence to the rules of bourgeois behavior. She knows, for example, who has waxed their floors and who buys wine, who has bought this item or that. "The Y's sent me a piece of cake; I'll have to take them some coffee." She once made friends with someone at work. "But I won't let her in my apartment," she told me. That would be more contact than she could stand. Worrying about the cleanliness of her apartment and her own body and worrying about her health absorb all her attention. Her living room is always picked up, always sterile. She knows where you can buy good sausage at a good price. But since consuming, even when it is done in company, does not create relationships, the gossip Mrs. K exchanges with other women in the shop never breaks out of the unreality and nonlife that is her life.

Living without religion means that she is cut off from others, an isolated individual. She has no past and no future. She feels no sympathy, no pangs of guilt, no self-doubt. She does not ask the big questions: Where are we going? Where do we come from? What meaning does life have, does my life have?

Mrs. S does not, of course, ask these questions in any explicit form either. But they are real for her nonetheless, because her life has so many more dimensions to it. When a boy from the neighborhood was killed in a motorcycle accident, she said, obviously addressing her question to God, "How could such a thing happen?" Responding to a similar incident, in which a boy was killed, Mrs. K said, "His parents had invested so much in him."

Here we can see, perhaps, what it is that forces me to speak of religion again and in a new way. It is this phenomenon of mass atheism, this a-religiosity rooted in banality. And this mass atheism has taken over without a struggle. No one had to fight for it against the powerful authority of church, school, or public opinion. It has taken over without anyone's being aware of its victory. The alternative to it has lost its force, its meaning, and become ridiculous.

Previous debate over religion did not concern itself much with this fact. It took place on a level of conscious discussion and decision. For my generation of theology students (I completed my university studies in 1954), the opposition was still a militant, conscious atheism that rejected religion in the interests of humanity. The fact that dialectical theology, unlike hardly any theology before it, tried to free itself

from "religion" follows logically from its clash with bour-
geois-liberal religiosity, which is most vividly symbolized in
the trivialization of the St. Matthew Passion. For dialectical
theology, this kind of religiosity gradually came to stand
for all religion, which was now rejected on theological
grounds. Mass atheism, the barren banality of the new
petit bourgeois a-religiosity, was not considered in the context of this discussion. The technological changes in the
production of consumer goods—changes that began to
take place in West Germany at about the same time as the
"economic miracle"—have given us a "consumer's heaven
on earth" (K.-W. Bühler) of which earlier critiques of religion could not have conceived and which has nothing whatsoever to do with Heine's wish "to possess here on earth
the kingdom of heaven." "Trivial religion in the age of
consumerism" has made human desires totally manipula-
ble. All desires to be different, to become a new being, to
relate differently to others, to communicate in a new way,
have been exchanged for the wish to possess things. It
makes a difference whether a person says at some point in
life, "Create in me a clean heart, O God, and put a new and
right spirit within me" (Ps. 51:10), or whether the yearnings that take this direction of radical change find no language in which to express themselves. These lines are not
promoting some bourgeois inner spirituality. Their context
speaks against such an interpretation. It simply states the
human desire to be other than one is ("renewed") and to
have a "right" spirit, a less vacillating one.

Mrs. K exemplifies how the profound and genuine
desires of human beings can be silenced and suffocated and
their passionate energies led off in the wrong directions.
"Consume!" becomes the categorical imperative that gov-
erns everyone's actions at all times.

In view of this total despiritualization of relationships,
we can say, comparatively speaking, that Mrs. S's desires
and expectations from life are infinitely higher than Mrs.

K's. Mrs. S's love of life, her participation in the vital force, goes infinitely farther than Mrs. K's. Pain and joy, wishes and fears are infinitely more profound in Mrs. S's life than they are in Mrs. K's.

"Banality is the counterrevolution" (Isaac Babel). Religion is a form of rebelling against individual and institutionalized banality. Religion sets off a special day, the Sabbath, a festival, against the everyday. To live without religion means for Mrs. K that there is no difference between Sundays and workdays and that there was no difference between them before, either, when her husband was still going to work. Religion sees divisions of time in the light of our desires for fulfillment. "Sometimes I'm up, sometimes I'm down, Oh, yes, Lord." Mrs. K does not sing. Mrs. S likes to sing songs that highbrows, in their unparalleled arrogance and condescension, might well refer to as sentimental trash.

Personal relationships and not just family ones play a central role in Mrs. S's life. She tells a visitor: "Why don't you go and have Alois cut your hair? He doesn't have much business these days. And have him give you a wash while you're at it." Direct perceptions of others, perceptions that are not filtered through a petit bourgeois system of values; greater physical awareness in one's dealings with others; sympathy; the qualities of someone capable of sympathy— these are the values that Mrs. S holds to and that are expressed for her in the medium of religion.

Almost all the positive figures in Heinrich Böll's stories live and move in this climate of communication, sympathy, and concern. Critics who were out to pinpoint something specifically religious in this Catholic author rarely found what they were looking for. In the climate of his novels, religion is simply an assumed presence, as is the assumption of meaning in life, an assumption from which people act and come into conflict. What is explicitly present is a healthy Catholic anticlericalism.

Religion is, as Emile Durkheim defined it, the self-valida-tion of a society by means of ritual practices and of myths that create meaning and integrate the society. The mythos includes an assurance of the divinity's proximity and a sense of special membership, of feeling oneself to be among the elect. The mythos is unfolded in dogma and in moral requirements, in the doctrine of a religion. Ritual is the solemn, communicative celebration in which the ascer-taining of meaning is symbolically realized, as in the acts of eating and drinking.

Myth and ritual are completely lacking in Mrs. K's life, unless we choose to regard certain views and acts of hers as substitutes for these things. But it is clear that there is an absence of myth in her consciousness. A life that amounts to more than just work is inconceivable to her. So, too, is ritual in the sense of a body language rich in gesture. In her life, there is no kneeling down, no standing up to sing, no movement that is as superfluous as making the sign of the cross over fresh bread.

Mrs. K's a-religiosity is a reduction, an impoverishment, a loss of human potential. She is unable to participate in myth and ritual, unable to integrate herself into a group.

Religion is, of course, only one factor in this complex system. The contrasts between village and city, extended family and nuclear family, are equally important and have a direct bearing on the question of religion. The two women I have described here are representative types whose lives illuminate our social history. In the course of further indus-trialization, urbanization, and secularization, Mrs. S's daughters and granddaughters will come to resemble Mrs. K more and more. Transcending everyday life and its pres-sures becomes increasingly difficult. The essence of a-religiosity, as I see it, is isolation; and isolation is becoming more and more prevalent. More and more people retire into a purely private life, in which the individual has no influence at all on even the most minute sector of public life and is at the mercy of a centralized bureaucracy. Work and consuming are in fact the only things that Mrs. K has ever known. For her, myth and ritual still exist only in atrophied or distorted form. An old Christian thesis that received considerable attention from the leaders of the Reformation says that where God is absent no vacuum develops but rather false gods work their mischief. People continue to "believe," and in everything they do they rely on God; they invent God; they "provide themselves with God," as Luther puts it. The question remains, however, which God this is, which relationships are seen as important, which values are promulgated in myth and reenacted and celebrated in ritual.

If we agree with this thesis, we then have to ask: In the framework of which myths and rituals does present-day a-religiosity exist? It is not easy to define the God of Mrs. K and of others like her, but the values that this God embodies are remnants of the Protestant work ethic: order, work, and health. The greatest gifts that this God can bestow are work, for which we have to be healthy (otherwise we become a burden on others), and a social order in which the state guarantees the continuance of this system. The ritual that people of Mrs. K's type engage in with almost religious ardor is, of course, a modern one, namely, shopping. Going to a department store is the equivalent of going to holy Mass. And this ritual has its rules: The shopper must be prepared, be well dressed, preferably have been at the hairdresser's. She has to know the hymns and prayers, this week's specials, how much who is charging for what. She is allowed to cheat a little and buy butter at shop X, even though at store Y . . . She can come home exhausted yet proud of the "little bargain" she managed to pick up. I have heard American women pronounce the word "shopping" with a zeal that sent cold chills down my spine.

Mrs. S's life is richer because it contains more of what

religion has always offered: transcendence. I will try to illustrate what I mean by this with one last political example. Mrs. K knows almost nothing about hunger in the world. Because she watches mainly comedies, talk shows, and detective stories on television, she is politically uninformed to a degree that people with a middle-class education can hardly conceive of. By contrast, Mrs. S hears about world hunger all the time through her church, her church's youth group, Catholic charitable organizations, and collections for starving people. She is capable of making a connection between what she hears about world hunger and her own experience at the end of World War II. Her memories remain an integral part of her life because she continues to have experiences that transcend the ego. Connectedness, not isolation, is what determines her thoughts and actions.

I can hardly imagine any support for political change developing in the consciousness of wage earners, of whom Mrs. K is representative, as long as the pain that individuals could feel is anesthetized by large doses of consumer goods. Blindness to the conflict between the First and Third Worlds is not likely to be cured where information, sympathy, and historical consciousness have been so thoroughly eradicated. Then, too, we have to realize that for social administrators and politicians, not to mention business interests, Mrs. K is a much more desirable type than Mrs. S. Because Mrs. S feels, communicates, and acts, she cannot be so easily manipulated. It is her type that will mess up the best-laid plans for construction of the next atomic power plant.

Over 95 percent of the farmers of Larzac in southern France who have been resisting development of an immense military base for the past seven years are Catholics who go to Mass on Sundays and who used to vote for the Right. Their resistance against a massive military machine backed up by weapons, police, politicians, and laws opened their eyes to struggles going on in other parts of the world. They formed an alliance with striking workers, and the workers helped them dig the ditch for an illegal water line so that the farmers "wouldn't have to go to jail again." When they learned that the military wanted their land to test weapons that would then be sold to Third World countries, they sent not weapons but 50,000 francs' worth of wheat to the Sahel region of Africa. They have fought their fight out of loyalty to the message of the gospel, acting from the kind of transcendence I have been trying to describe here. One of their nonviolent, symbolic acts was to plow up some army land and plant 103 trees where the military had planned to locate production for death. And next to the trees, they rolled into place a huge block of stone to represent their determined, tenacious resistance. As a song from the American protest movement says, clearly alluding to the First Psalm: "Like the tree that's rooted by the waters/ we shall not be moved."

This shepherds' protest movement in Larzac is one among many that have caught the attention of scholars in America and been grouped together under the heading "people's religion." A rediscovery and reevaluation of authentic folk religion is under way both here and in America, and this effort cannot be dismissed as merely "romantic," even though present European solidarity with the nearly eradicated Indians of both North and South America bears some resemblance to the eighteenth-century poet Hölderlin's enthusiasm for the Greek freedom fighters of his time.

The religion, the customs, the language, the songs, and —perhaps most important of all—the resistance and struggle of the people are assuming a new importance in the face of urbanization, secularization, and the overly cerebral theology of the theologians. "Black theology" cannot be understood without taking into account its roots in the piety of black people, in their spirituals, and in the achievements of the black freedom fighters whose history has so often been hushed up or distorted. This is also true of the Puerto Rican freedom movement, which finds its strongest expression in music and in what the ruling schools of theology and sociology choose to call a "sect." In a reggae concert I once heard some musicians sing only one word for about six minutes straight. They stuttered this word, groaned it, drummed it, screamed it, sang it, choked it out, shrieked it: Africa, Africa! Probably none of these young musicians had any "real" tie to the old continent or a currently accurate picture of it. But none of them would admit, either, that they could live without this cry that expresses yearning, despair, humiliation, rage, hatred, victory, and the reclaiming of what they had lost; that they could live without this mythology. In view of the growing economic disparities in the world today, the old observation that the poor have always been more pious than the rich is truer than ever.

My fear of people who are isolated and dead and my interest in the simplest forms of transcendence, forms almost unattainable for the middle class, constitute, then, a taking of sides with those people who in their oppression have made "religion" a term of liberation. They have taken myth away from the kings and their officials and readapted it for those whose path through life would be no easier than the one that led from a stinking stall to a torture instrument of class justice; that is, the path that led from the manger to the cross.

Do these observations contain a faint spark of religious and political hope? Is the destruction of connectedness, which is a necessary historical stage in freedom from religion, a sign of progress? Is modern mass atheism, to which suffering and struggle are alien, as inevitable as the electric light? Do traditional types like Mrs. S have to be trimmed down to petit bourgeois size so that perhaps the generations that follow Mrs. K will once again, through better education and greater awareness, have the possibility of greater connectedness with life?

It is hard for me to believe that anything positive can come from isolation, from an existence devoid of religion and communication. Faced with Mrs. K's despair, my sense is that this is the absolute end. Her despair is worse than anything you'll find in a psychiatric hospital.

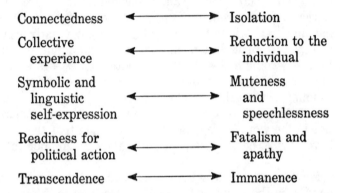

Connectedness	←——————→	Isolation
Collective experience	←——————→	Reduction to the individual
Symbolic and linguistic self-expression	←——————→	Muteness and speechlessness
Readiness for political action	←——————→	Fatalism and apathy
Transcendence	←——————→	Immanence

This is not the kind of immanence that the nineteenth-century critics of religious transcendence had in mind. But today we are seeing the consequences of disconnectedness reflected more and more in mass phenomena and everyday life.

Religion can be described as a generous, all-inclusive gesture of unification. Its point is to be at one with everything that lives. Becoming one with all life and leaving our particular existence behind is what we practice in ritual and in prayer.

It was not at this suspension of individual and particular existence that early bourgeois and industrial-proletarian critiques of religion were aimed. On the contrary, the possibility for generalization that particular interests have was an inherent premise in the pathos of humanity. In its intent, the socialist movement has always been oriented toward humanity as a whole.

The Preface of the Roman Catholic liturgy expresses this becoming-at-one in liturgical formulations that go back to that great mystic of the early church, Dionysius the Areopagite. The congregation prays—with all Christendom, with the heavens and the seraphim—"Holy, holy, holy." "And so we [the local congregation] sing with the angels and archangels [the heavenly congregation], with the dominions and powers [cosmic beings in the heavenly spheres], and with all the heavenly hosts [of all time] the praise of thy glory and cry out without ceasing: Holy, holy, holy . . ."

Berdyaev remarked that human beings are incurably religious, and with that famous quote in mind, I would say in somewhat more cautious terms that being cut off from transcendence destroys people psychically and socially, destroys them beyond all cure. I realize that we cannot just simply sing the Sanctus again, but perhaps it is my task in these dark times to keep alive at least the desire to sing with everyone, including the dead, including the cosmos. The position of the rich white middle class in a world of starving people is one of disconnectedness. We have built a wall out of weapons and the dictatorship of capital. By comparison to this wall, the Berlin Wall is a mere bagatelle. A reunification with the human hopes and struggles in which we, behind our wall, have no part would be a step toward what Ernst Bloch has called "transcending without transcendence." Rebellion against banality, against a production-line society, against isolation and disconnectedness contains in itself the potential for liberation of all religions. "Less than All cannot satisfy Man" (William Blake).

2
LIFE WITHOUT SUFFERING— A UTOPIA?

From time immemorial, the idea of a life free of suffering has been a myth, a utopian dream, a religious hope. Today, in the industrialized countries that are geared to consumerism, social reality is such that the avoidance of suffering has become an attainable goal, one that is taken for granted and requires no further discussion. As Leszek Kolakowski says in his *Gegenwärtigkeit des Mythos* (Presentness of Myth), "One of the most important though rarely articulated characteristics of our civilization is the total rejection of belief in the value of suffering." Kolakowski goes on to describe our world as a "culture of analgesics" and speaks of a "headlong flight from suffering," a "narcotizing of life." Apathy, an absence of suffering, and the desire to go through life without experiencing pain are all hallmarks of the culture dominant in the First World.

We are in a position, it seems, to do away with the objective causes of suffering, which appears to be almost a fossil from prehistoric times. Greater access to information and education, increased mobility, and the weakening of our primary human ties relieve us of many forms of suffering. We can assume that the pain and difficulties people experience in a divorce, for example, will decrease in the future and that psychic and social pain will be reduced in the same way that physical pain has been reduced. This will not be achieved solely through pills or other medicines that anesthetize us and make us forget; it will also happen because the objective reasons for psychic pain will become fewer. We will be spared social suffering just as we are spared physical suffering. In a society where the possibility of new contacts is always open, the loss of a marriage partner will be less painful than in one where contact is severely limited. Our greater geographical and social mobility plays an important role in this. Frequent moves and job changes accustom people to situations of parting. Fewer and fewer ties can be regarded as bonds for life, and as a consequence, the breaking of ties does not evoke the same kind of pain it did in the past. Possibilities for contact have increased, and it has become easier to transfer feelings from one person to another. We experience the loss of a friend or partner less acutely, and frequent changes in relationships induce a dulling of the pain that such losses involve. But as our capacity to feel pain is reduced, our human relationships lose the depth that characterized them in earlier cultures.

"The narcotizing of life," Kolakowski writes, "is the enemy of human community. The more incapable we become of bearing our own suffering, the easier it becomes for us to ignore the suffering of others." This describes perfectly the double aspect of apathy: denial and repression of one's own suffering and icy indifference to the suffering of others. We refuse to think about death and the questions it poses. We avoid love, which, as Kolakowski says, "often tends to be a source of suffering." And this very remoteness in our intimate relationships, this strategy for avoiding pain, is part and parcel of that massive indifference with which we witness the eradication of other peoples. Anyone who has tried even once to hand out leaflets during shopping hours in any German city will know just what I am talking about. Responses to a questionnaire distributed among foreign visitors in West Germany identified "a certain coldness in human relationships" as the most striking characteristic of the German middle class. Apathy as the denial of suffering in one's own inner life, apathy as the incapacity to feel sympathy for others.

The problem of apathy—the apathy of the white middle class in the First World—is perhaps the most telling example we can find to demonstrate the truth of the slogan from the women's movement that says, The personal is the political. The inability to feel one's own suffering, the repression of suffering, and the incapacity to perceive the suffering of others are all aspects of that apathy, and the concept of apathy may eventually prove to be the one we will draw on to circumscribe that new psychosocial quality that has been known ever since Marx's early writings as "alienation." When sympathy is linked with crime and made to appear as criminal, as has been done in West Germany in recent years, then what other name can we give to the attitude the state fosters among its citizens but apathy?

The old Christian desire for the utopia of a life without suffering, for that time when "the dwelling of God is with men. He will dwell with them. . . . He will wipe away every tear from their eyes"—this desire can be understood today only if we consider it in relationship to this apathy I have been describing, an apathy that is technologically produceable, that is desired by our governments, and that is affirmed by our culture. I am drawing here on the book of

Revelation, but we cannot, either in this case or any other, simply quote the Bible and assume that the expectations and desires of the many groups described in it are identical with our own. This kind of cheap appropriating of the Bible and empathizing with it is grotesque, as if the questions and longings expressed there were the same as "ours," as if people who probably haven't cried since they were children and who have to be moved to thirst by advertising had the slightest claim to the promise in Revelation 21:4 that "death shall be no more, neither shall there be mourning nor crying nor pain any more."

The people who were waiting for the city of God were the disinherited and the masses who had been deprived of their rights. They clearly had a genuine interest in seeing that "the first heaven and the first earth had passed away" and that an unjust world was brought to justice. "They who have come out of the great tribulation" (Rev. 7:14) were Christians persecuted by the Roman government. And throughout the history of biblical exegesis and appropriation, the people who have always called out for a God who "will wipe away every tear" were those who were oppressed and persecuted, like the Montanists in the second century and the German peasants in the sixteenth, people who were deprived to an intolerable degree of their right to life and of the possibilities of life.

The first thing we have to do, then, is place our inquiry in its proper geographical and historical context. Who were these people who hoped for this particular end to history and who conceived of Christian utopia as life without suffering? Where and when did these hopes arise? By stating our question in these terms, we set a materialistic exegesis of the Bible against an idealistic and generalizing one. The writers of the Bible did not write for "humanity" or some other abstract entity. Bourgeois theology, of course, manages to put its own interpretation even on the book of Revelation. It overlooks Judgment and the necessary fact that "the first heaven and the first earth" will have to pass before the tears of the afflicted can be wiped away. Bourgeois theology reduces the utopian hope to a private affair, as though it were promised to every individual regardless of what palace of injustice that individual happens to be living in, even if only as a doorkeeper or a cleaning woman.

Life without hunger is promised to the hungry, not to the overfed. "And death shall be no more" is a promise made to those who die of the flu at two or twelve or, to use the statistician's figure, at thirty-two because they are malnourished. Revelation does not promise freedom from suffering for everyone. It promises only that justice will finally be attained for those who have been destroyed.

This brings me back to my point of departure. The state of permanent, built-in injustice we contribute to and benefit from in this society has, of course, consequences for our system of values. We have inverted the relationship between love and suffering, turning upside down the hierarchical order in which they stand. Our highest goal, recognized as such by almost everyone, is to be free of suffering, to become free of it and remain free of it right up to the moment of death. Health is, as we all know, the highest good. To be alive, to transcend the ego, to be in communication and sympathy with everything that lives, all this is subordinated to freedom from suffering. This apathetic freedom from suffering, this freedom from want and from pain and from commitment to people and causes has been promoted to our highest value, along with flawless beauty, unblemished cleanliness, uninterrupted advancement in one's career, all those qualities that separate our style of life so markedly from that of other peoples. The goals of being capable of love and of bringing about justice are subordinated to the goal of getting through life "well," which is to say getting through unscathed, untouched.

To speak of "inversion" and of a "hierarchical order" is to use very conservative language. The fact is that I strongly disapprove of a moral relativism that shies away from such evaluations. The fact is that "freedom from suffering" is only of secondary value and is not the goal Jesus Christ strove for. If we are able to envision Christian utopia only in negative terms, defining it as the absence of suffering, then our definition may be fit for stones and computers, but for human beings and for God-become-man it is inadequate. This is why utopia is obliged to leave the language of concepts behind and adopt the language of images. Once we realize this, it becomes clear that the city of God, the heavenly Jerusalem, means more than "life without suffering."

We have to guard against facile theological interpretations of suffering. From a Christian point of view, suffering does not exist in order to break our pride, demonstrate our impotence, or take advantage of our dependency. The purpose of suffering is not to lead us back to a God who attains to his greatness only by reducing us to insignificance.

It is surely a wretched theology that conceives of God as a sadist who can achieve his ends or find his pleasure only in making human beings suffer, though this kind of theology continues to haunt many a sermon and theological interpretation. "Suffering comes from God's hand." We come across this sentence, or others like it, time and again. It makes suffering seem inevitable and change through suffering impossible. It understands suffering as a trial that God imposes on us and that we have to endure, as a punishment that follows on past sins but is out of all proportion to them, or as a process of purification from which we will emerge cleansed.

There is some element of truth to these interpretations, but they do not begin to answer the truly important question, which is how we move from mere passive endurance of suffering to productive suffering. How do we rid ourselves of that deeply rooted desire to come through unscathed and to persist in imperturbed narcissism? How do we transform that desire into the wishes that are in fact expressed in Revelation 21?

Let's assume that God is not a sadist. That is, of course, in view of world history and of the individual fates that the most innocent have suffered, the least likely assumption we can make. And it is this unlikelihood that has convinced many people of the absurdity of faith. But let's go a step further. If God really is not a sadist, then he is also not responsible for visiting the plague on us or for approving construction of the neutron bomb. He is not an independent omniscient ruler, a contriver of suffering, an originator of it and a spectator to it. If God is not like this, then we should rid ourselves of this idea of an isolated, apathetic God who stands above all history. Anyone who continues to identify with isolation and the absence of suffering, with power and strength, with the protection, preservation, and salvation of self, that person may want to continue honoring such a God and paying homage to him with daily analgesics (the market offers a wide variety of choices in that line).

But if we assume that God is not in fact cynical, then he is not the great creator of suffering who deals out punishment and ordeals. He is instead the liberator, the ally of the poor. He is the oppressed victim, the man of sorrows. Then we are free to choose Jesus, who at the beginning of his work renounced both power and freedom from suffering when he was tempted by the devil. He did not want to be stronger than we are collectively. Or, to put it differently, he did not want to be strong except through the solidarity of the weak. Then and only then will we reach that point where the goal of "life without suffering" overcomes narcissism and replaces apathy with sympathy. Ceasing to be a mere utopian dream realizable only at the end of history, it becomes a way of experiencing the present. Then we will see, as John did on Patmos, that everything is very good, good for us too, even in these times.

3
LOVE YOUR NEIGHBOR
AS YOURSELF

"That certainly would be nice," my skeptical old friend said when I began questioning her about love for one's fellowman. Her response was something like Gandhi's when he was asked what he thought about Western culture. "It would be a wonderful idea," he said. It really would be nice, the idea that human beings on this planet were joined together in love, that they found their life's fulfillment in love, not in money or power. Just suppose that what people needed, what everything depended on and ultimately amounted to, what we learned our whole lives long, what we drew our sustenance from, what we were intended for long before we were born, and what will become of us when we are no longer here—let's just suppose that the last, final, ultimate reality we partook of in our daily traffic with each other were circumscribed by this one impossible (because much too great) word "love." That really would be nice.

"Love your neighbor; he is like you." Martin Buber's translation of the biblical command is rhythmically stronger than the traditional one. The pause in the middle of the sentence makes us think. And this reflection is not blurred by the altogether inappropriate question of what self-love really is and whether I can really love myself or not. Love of self and love of others are not compared. Working on a deeper level, this translation points to their common root, which is equality. Love your neighbor; he or she is like you. Be brotherly toward your neighbor because he or she is your equal. Among unequals there is only condescension, not love. It is in love's own interest to create equality so that it will be able to love. And that is why God created us in his own image, so that he would have something to love. Our love assumes likeness in others, even if we cannot see the likeness—as in the face of a criminal—but can only believe in it.

I want to single out and describe here three essential elements of love: giving and taking, attentiveness, and pain. The concept "love of others" denotes a relationship between people and not the virtue of any single person. (Traditionally, this point has been reflected in the designation of love for others as a "supernatural" or theological virtue. It is self-evident that what is supernatural cannot be possessed or acquired by individuals. The supernatural virtues—faith, hope, and charity—are concepts that describe life itself, that tell us what it means to live life to the full. They are relational concepts, concepts of connectedness.) Love is a mutual giving and taking. That does not mean that in every phase of a relationship the giver is also a taker. The good Samaritan gives what he has without receiving anything right back. But by giving without asking for anything in return he creates what I would like to call a net of neighborly love, a sense that nothing we do for each other is lost or done in vain. He puts his faith in giving and taking, even though, at the moment, he does nothing but give. Perhaps at some point in his past, during his childhood, he did nothing but take. The image of a net strikes me as apt because I want to suggest with it the relative security that giving and taking provide. The net holds us up. Granted, there are some holes in it, and people sometimes fall out of it into an emptiness where giving and taking are no longer possible. But this net of giving and taking is part of our daily experience. Every time we learn to give without calculating what we will get in return and every time we learn to receive without feeling ashamed or indebted, we tie a few more knots into this large net and make it a little more secure. Give to your neighbor; he or she will give as you do. Take from your neighbor; he or she has needs as you do. The basis of equality is that all of us have to give and all of us have to receive. ("You all came as tiny children to this world full of wind. Nobody called you, you were not asked, when a woman wrapped you in a diaper." Bertolt Brecht, *Domestic Breviary*.)

But is this really true? What, for example, can a bunch of stupid and arrogant students "give" me? The answer is, of course, nothing, as long as I insist on describing them in these terms. My error lies in my assumption that I, as the teacher, can give them something without also taking. Captive to this illusion, I cannot give them anything at all, not even information, much less the kind of insights that can transform people.

If I cease to take and to give, I become a stone. If I blossom as a tree blossoms, I am in an equilibrium of giving and taking. This is why the sentence "It is more blessed to give than to receive" is, in a profound sense, untrue and misleading. Perhaps we should say instead: It is more blessed to give and receive than to have and hold. If my hands are fully occupied in holding on to something, I can neither give nor receive.

To learn this equilibrium or mutuality of love, we have to develop a certain kind of concentration that Simone Weil has called "attentiveness." When we talk about learning to love, what we really have to learn is to attend to the reality of another person. We often see only what we are giving and tend, like a bad teacher, to overlook what we are receiving. We are inattentive to the reality of others the instant we regard them as objects that can satisfy our needs or desires, the instant we consider them from the standpoint of their utility to us. Attentiveness is a critical, negative force that blocks out our prejudices, expectations, and preconceived notions so that we become empty and ready to perceive what another person is expressing with the language of physical movements, gestures, and words. The Gospels, taken as a whole, constitute a single and often inadequate attempt to describe Jesus' attentiveness, an attentiveness that is the essential precondition for working miracles; and when we talk about love, what we are really talking about is the working of miracles.

But there is still a third element of neighborly love that I would like to discuss. Attentiveness leads us to giving and taking, makes us aware that we take part in giving and taking. But the more we give ourselves up to this process of giving and taking, the more inevitable the experience of pain becomes. I realize that this is a very Christian description of neighborly love, but I think it is one that humanists and Marxists can still find tolerable. Its critical intent is directed against behavioristic philosophy and psychology, which have outlawed pain as a kind of immaturity. In Christian terms, pain is inseparable from love. Jesus wept over his city of Jerusalem. Giving and taking reach their limitations. The net of love proves to be riddled with holes. Some people fall through them and are no longer accessible to us. Innumerable rational arguments are mustered on behalf of neighborly love, arguments that stress human self-interest and the idea of mutual aid. But there is also an irrational, paradoxical core to love that makes fools of us all; and as fools we know more of pain. We know that we will never get love under control, that we will always be in its debt, that it is ridiculous to say, "I did my best," because only someone who has given his life is justified in saying that. That we always remain behind love, can never catch up with it, is the definition of messianic pain in an unredeemed world. I would like to be a blossoming tree that lives in giving and taking and is attentive to the earth and the sun. But it is pain that separates me from these my brothers and sisters. We cannot demonstrate this pain for someone. It comes as an experience of faith, just as the realization that I am a sinner has to be believed in the light of the love that we fall behind and cannot reach.

To become attentive, to give and to take, not to deny pain —these are elaborations on that old text: Love your neighbor; he or she is like you. "That certainly would be nice," my skeptical friend said. But, as Brecht put it, the circumstances just aren't that way. Is not my description of love blind to the real difficulties love encounters, deaf to the causes of misery? What point is there in talking about love under capitalistic conditions? Shouldn't we speak of its failure instead? I do not mean that from a moral point of view, not in the sense that the demands of love are too great and we humans too weak and self-preoccupied. I mean it in a social sense. Is there not at the top of every page of newsprint, in invisible ink, the message: Love does not work? I saw a book title recently: *Love Alone Is Not Enough*, and a quote: "There is no true life in a false one." What we experience continually is the objective, and therefore subjective, impossibility of love.

Ignazio Silone tells a story from his childhood in Italy in which a poor woman suffers injustice. One Sunday morning, a landowner sics his dog on her, just for fun, as she is coming out of church. The dog knocks her down, tears her clothes, and injures her. She takes the feudal dog owner to court, but she can find no witnesses to testify for her even though many people saw the incident. The landowner claims she provoked the dog into attacking her. She loses her case and has to pay all the costs. Silone tells this story to illustrate the key experience of his childhood and youth. He describes this experience as "the massive contradiction, the incomprehensible, absurd, monstrous contradiction," between family and private life on the one hand and larger social relations on the other. In the private sphere, life is conducted decently, honorably, and in accordance with the commandment of love; but in the social sphere, Silone finds human relations horrible, dominated by hatred and deceit. The judge who finds the woman guilty admits in private how sorry he feels about the case, but as a judge he has to remain objective. Silone reflects on this inconsistency between private decency, the capacity for sympathy and love for one's neighbor, and public indifference and hypocrisy. The woman advises her young son never to become a judge. "Keep away from that kind of stuff and stay at home." The rules that hold in the family and are taught in catechism do not apply outside the familial realm. Love your neighbor, but not in public. Love has become a private affair and nothing more. Giving and taking, the net of trust, attentiveness to others, and the pain of the mother who is aware of the horror her son feels—it is all there but has no bearing on relationships outside the family.

In our country, some of the monstrous abuses of a feudal judicial system have been overcome, but that basic division between private and public morality, between the family and the world of work and business, between the personal and the social, has, if anything, grown deeper. It has never been easy to love one's neighbor, but in our situation has it not become an objective impossibility? A working woman in the electronics industry, a woman who is a good mother to her children, does not even know that the little gadgets she produces for eight hours every day will eventually be incorporated into weapons designed to kill someone else's children. A young teacher who comforts and nurtures her own child at home works in school in a gigantic sorting machine, calculates the value of children in points, and communicates to them the amount of pressure prescribed for them by the school authorities. The number of children in her classroom and the pressures of the curriculum objectively prevent her from developing what I have called the attentiveness of love. It is her job to strip her pupils, at an early age, of their readiness to help others, their sympathy, their solidarity, so that she can make them able to perform and compete. There is no room for giving and taking. The pressure to achieve destroys this natural structure. The young teacher is in effect two separate people. Only at home can she make attempts at loving.

The concept of the neighbor, a concept from an older, agrarian world, is dead. Love, which a Catholic dictionary defines as the capacity to seek out others for their own sake and not for any use they can be to us, has become restricted to the private sphere. Contemporary philosophy has known this for a long time and has registered it in its systems theory. This theory distinguishes between different systems such as the state, the economy, science, and the family; and it assigns love to the sphere of the family. Just as money is the province of the economy and truth the province of science and scholarship, so love is the province of the family (Niklas Luhmann). Within this division of life, love is allowed only a small sphere of influence. Other very real aspects of human relationships are regulated by quite different laws and sanctions.

The fate that love has undergone in the bourgeois world is one of reduction. Love is no longer capable of defining human relationships meaningfully or regulating them satisfactorily. In a neighborly, agrarian world, it still could do those things. In such a world, the command to love your neighbor was rooted in giving and taking, in mutual aid. It meant: Help your neighbor; he or she is no better off than you. You are as subject to plague, drought, or a band of robbers as your neighbor is. This was a rational rule of thumb, not an impossibly excessive demand. What has happened to love in the last two hundred years is that a relatively rational, universal principle of mutual aid, rooted in rational self-interest, has evolved into a feeling that now holds sway only in a limited sector. That sensible phrase "as yourself" becomes less and less comprehensible. Excessive demands, unrealistic thinking, and sentimentality are the hallmarks of those apostles of love who want to heal the world's ills with more neighborly love from one person to another. Our modern Christmas celebration is an appalling manifestation of this development. Giving and taking are reduced to an exchange of things; attentiveness is destroyed; and pain is sentimentalized. In capitalism, love occurs (a) within the family and (b) at Christmas.

Can something that has become objectively irrelevant still retain subjective validity for the individual? I would guess that the deepest hopes of the bourgeoisie were invested in proving that it could; and, compared with the cynicism prevalent today, that attempt was a brave and generous effort. Love, humanity, closeness, and warmth were confined to a small sphere; they were acted out and passed on primarily by women whose historical and cultural role it was to work with this reduced form of love. "There is true life in a false one" was the major thesis of the bourgeoisie. My grandparents probably still believed in it. I speak out of sadness and confusion, not to denounce anyone. It took a long time for love to keep shrinking and shrinking until no one could really believe in its reality anymore—in what Marx called its worldliness and its power—and my Jewish friend said, "It certainly would be nice." For in the long run what has become objectively impossible, meaningless, and empty in society cannot be maintained subjectively; and the attempt to put the values we orient our lives around into two separate compartments has failed. The loving fathers who ran the gas chambers in Auschwitz symbolize the dreadful end of this bourgeois experiment. In the novels of the last twenty years we find described in the clearest of terms how the objective impossibility of love and mutual aid thwarts even subjective attempts to experience and create love, as in attempts to humanize sexuality. We see men making desperate efforts to become human, in bed if nowhere else. In a world that takes objective, that is to say, technological, economic, and political cognizance of no other objects than those that are utilitarian or that satisfy desires, in a world that has reduced the range of human activities to nothing but production and consumption, in a world in which giving and taking have been reduced to buying and selling, the attentiveness of love cannot even emerge, much less grow. Institutions like the family and the church, shot through as they are with what Marx called their drivel about love, destroy the language of love. In this situation, one in which love has been reduced to a private, powerless, and sentimental affair, new and better designs for a human life are essential. As I see it, two possibilities are open to us.

The first I would call the technocratic solution. The case its spokesmen make runs something like this: It is pointless to ask people to love their neighbors. This Judeo-Christian dream is passé. Rational modes of life that avoid pain, modes that B. F. Skinner, for example, has described, replace our old excessive demands and sentimental yearnings. Love your neighbor is not a false directive but simply a meaningless one in the sense that it contains no real prescriptions for action. The religious outlook inherent in this imperative, namely, the assumption that in loving we not only do something beautiful and valuable but also participate in the meaning of life, becoming a living part of that totality which used to be called by that old word "God" —this outlook wakens excessive expectations from life.

What human beings need is not love; their needs are as subject to planning and manipulation as anything else.

The most inclusive term I can find to describe the other possibility is the "humanistic solution." Its spokesmen are Jews, Christians, humanists, and socialists. The traditional family squabbles between these brothers, who are in some respects very different from each other, seem less significant to me than that great quarrel they have with all those who consider any discussion of love totally irrelevant. Love your neighbor; he or she is like you. In the humanistic tradition, that imperative represents more than just a fond dream of humankind. Love is perhaps the deepest need that people have; learning to give and to receive, their greatest task. It is not just the fulfillment of this need that is threatened today and that has always been threatened. What is threatened now is cognizance of this need, the very fact of its existence. There is no longer any general consensus on what human beings need or on whether they might not do much better with something less than love. To circumscribe our deepest human needs, our tradition has used the word "soul," expressing in that word our failings, our dreams, and our hopes. Is there really such a thing as the human soul, or is the soul simply an invention of the Judeo-Christian tradition, something that is kept alive by remnants of our traditional upbringing?

The debate between these two factions is not over. Should we conclude from the failure of love that has been reduced to private relationship that our need for love is not a genuine need? Or may we hope that love which does not reside solely within the family and is not willing to forego justice has future possibilities that we, at the end of the bourgeois era, are not yet able to perceive. Is the technocratic solution that declares our deepest needs unreal and tries to manipulate them out of existence the only solution? Or can we conceive of a society that takes these needs more seriously than all past eras have because it seeks to establish giving and taking on a different economic basis for all people.

I would like to close with a Jewish story. An old rabbi once asked his students how one could recognize the time when night ends and day begins. "Is it when, from a great distance, you can tell a dog from a sheep?" one student asked. "No," said the rabbi. "Is it when, from a great distance, you can tell a date palm from a fig tree?" another student asked. "No," said the rabbi. "Then when is it?" the students asked. "It is when you look into the face of any human creature and see your brother or your sister there. Until then, night is still with us."

4
MARY IS A SYMPATHIZER

Mary—the first image that comes to my mind is the plaster figure in the grotto at Lourdes, her eyes lowered, the outlines of her body lost in the endless folds of her robe: desexualized and humble, the feminine ideal, a symbol created to teach self-oppression to the oppressed, self-censure to the self-critical, self-exploitation to the doubly exploited.

This ploy works best if the idol appears to be elevated, raised up on a pedestal and glorified. Just as the image of the loyal, self-sacrificing Uncle Tom was an integral part of the oppression of blacks, so the image of a sublime and elevated Mary was integral to the oppression of women. She is enthroned above us. She is pure; we are filthy. She is desexualized; we have sexual needs and problems. We can never measure up to her and should therefore feel guilty and ashamed. And that, in turn, makes us feel all the more humble.

Mary's submission was voluntary. "Let it be to me according to your word" is her response to an unwanted pregnancy (Luke 1:38). She accepts deprivation and pain; she serves without complaint. She has no will of her own. She is the Lord's handmaiden. And even if we cannot be "pure" like her, we can at least be as submissive as she is.

Raising someone up on a pedestal is a strategy of domination. Women are glorified, elevated, and praised so that they can be humiliated, restricted, and blocked at every turn. The inevitable reverse image of the madonna is the whore. *Finalmente siamo donne, non piu putane, non piu madonne!* (We are women, not whores or madonnas!) This is one of the slogans of the women's movement in Italy. And it is no coincidence that the feminists of a Catholic country are so outspoken in opposing the mindless alternative of "whore or saint." But is Mary really this plaster figure, a girl from Nazareth with an illegitimate son who was later executed as a revolutionary? Was it this Mary who appeared to the peasant girl Joan of Arc and entrusted to her that most masculine of instruments, the sword?

Is submission really the theme of that passage in the Bible in which Mary celebrates her pregnancy? The passage is utterly unequivocal in its distinction between the lowly and the high and mighty, between the poor and the rich, utterly clear about the impotence of the unpropertied classes in relation to the powers that be, the helplessness of those who are without rights because they are without property.

And Mary said,
   "My soul magnifies the Lord,
   and my spirit rejoices in God my Savior. . . .
   He has shown strength with his arm,

he has scattered the proud in the imagination of
    their hearts,
he has put down the mighty from their thrones,
and exalted those of low degree;
he has filled the hungry with good things,
and the rich he has sent empty away."

(Luke 1:46–53)

The people who have turned to Mary—and women in
particular—have thought, desired, and hoped for very different things in different periods. The desexualization that
culminated in the breastless, bloodless plaster noblewoman
of Lourdes is the outgrowth of a development in art history
that began in the Renaissance and reached its high point
in the nineteenth century. This is the bourgeois period, and
it was the theology of this particular class that inspired the
image of a humble, desexualized Mary.

In the Middle Ages, for example, depictions of Mary are
more sensual, lively, and cheerful. She is shown nursing
her baby, her breasts bared and beautiful. She is shown
changing his diapers and bouncing him on her knee. She is
also shown crying out with pain or numbed by grief as she
mourns her son who has been tortured to death. There are
paintings that show her taking leave of him as he sets out
into the world. She knows perhaps better than he what lies
before him. (My God, I wish that my relationship with my
son were characterized by their kind of "communication
without domination," by that kind of warmth, understanding of each other, closeness, pain, trust!) There are other
Marys quite different from the submissive one. The one
that first comes to mind, of course, is the great mother who
comforts and protects. The Catholic tradition took from her
her other children who are mentioned in the Bible, but the
people's needs and fantasies have given these children
back to her, shoving them in under her skirts, as it were,
where they find shelter from hail and rain, from pestilence
and war.

Very early on, Mary assumed the role as a protector not only against the forces of nature but also those of a violent society. She did not embody "justice" as our society understands it and practices it today. That is, she did not operate on the principle that everyone should get what he or she deserves, a principle that leaves inequality of opportunity intact. No, Mary embodied mercy, or what we usually call "charity." I am a bit uneasy with this word, but I cannot find a better one. What I mean to say is that Mary rejects "performance" as a measure of human value. I will not stick by you, she says, because you are handsome, clever, successful, musical, potent, or whatever. I'll stick by you without reservations or conditions. I'll stick by you because you are there, because you need me. Her unconditional acceptance is that of a mother who cannot exchange her child in the store if she finds it doesn't suit her. If we strip charity of sentimentality, the "amoral" quality it originally had becomes visible again. And it is for this kind of amorality that the Mary of legends and folk tales has a mischievous penchant.

Until well into the High Middle Ages, Mary was not a particularly popular figure in the liturgy, in dogmatic writings, and in literature under the influence of the clergy. She belonged to the poor, the unlettered, the mendicant friars, the people. She was known as the "madonna of rogues," which is to say the madonna of the impoverished rural proletariat, who could not help being at odds with the increasingly stringent laws that defined and protected property. A Polish legend tells about a robber who calls on Mary for aid just before the hangman puts the noose around his neck. Mary hastens to him, stands under the gallows, and supports the hanged man's feet for three days and three nights. Presumed dead, the robber is cut down from the gallows, only to run off, rendering thanks to the Virgin. The heroes of such legends are often thieves and robbers—or monks and nuns who have fled the rigors of monastery or cloister—people who oppose law and order and that masculine set of mind intent on domination and regulation. When a "fallen" abbess gives birth to a child, Mary attends her as a midwife. When a nun runs away from the cloister, Mary takes her place for years at the cloister's prayer services.

This kind of subversive activity is bound to bring Mary into religious conflict with God the Father and with Christ. Mary subverts the division of people into sheep and goats. This anarchistic tendency of hers has never been completely eradicated, and a Protestant encyclopedia has this indignant comment to make on such folk legends: "These stories are infused with a rather peculiar morality" (*Die Religion in Geschichte und Gegenwart,* 2d ed., 1927).

The figure of Mary, then, is as ambiguous as all religious concepts and symbols. She serves the interests of religiously glorified submissiveness but also those of consolation, protection, and the rescue of victims. Mary is submissive, but she is also subversive in the way police in Latin America use this word: She undermines the power of the ruling classes. To use a term that has been used widely in West Germany recently, we could say that Mary is a sympathizer.*

The little madonna who spoke of liberation in the passage quoted from Luke is not made of plaster or plastic. She is very much alive, alive in the history of all who are oppressed, alive in the history of women. The only reason we know so little of the dreams, visions, and stories of those who fight and resist is that history has been written by the victors.

In Latin America, the *madonna leone* rides naked on

---

*TRANSLATORS' NOTE: The term *Sympathisant* was used widely in the German press in the mid-1970s in connection with reports on terrorist activity. The term suggested that anyone with leftist political convictions "sympathized" with terrorism and was guilty by association.

the back of a lion and—at least for our tamed and corrupted sense of religion—appears to be more witch than saint. In the late Middle Ages, the rebellious peasants who wanted to give the land back to the people who actually cultivated it gathered under the aegis of Mary.

And that brings me to a new and better image of the girl Mary: impudent as Joan of Orleans, who dared to tell an archbishop to his face that what he had just said was, "even for him, unusually stupid." Seen in this light, Mary is no longer just a tamed, subdued woman but also a rebellious girl. Militance and charity are united in her, and she becomes an image of hope for those who have been cheated of their lives.

At the same time, however, she has always been a model that repressive forces have held up to women to keep them humble and in their place. This is why Catholic cultures in particular have been so ready to cast off and forget this double-sided figure.

Personally, though, I take a rather skeptical view of any kind of throwaway society. I cannot put any trust in an existence that is presumably free of images and myths. We have seen it happen that where old images are put aside, new ones in no respect more enlightened take their place. In the niche once occupied by the untainted madonna, we now find a Mrs. Whiter-than-White from the detergent ads. Both ideologies force onto women a role that weakens and cripples them.

Like many Christians in the liberation movement, I am not ready to surrender Mary to our opponents. The suggestion that we forget Mary and religion as quickly as we can strikes me as hasty and simplistic. Contemporary liberation movements need their patron saints and models, too; they need to be rooted in history. Merely to rid ourselves of the Lourdes madonna, then, is to achieve nothing at all.

I find it hard to think that the millions of women before me who have loved Mary were simply blind or duped. They, too, must have offered resistance, resistance from which we can learn.

5
ON THE OPPRESSION
OF MEN

Speaking about the "oppression of men" poses certain difficulties for me. It seems to me that the place where people in our society experience their lack of freedom most clearly is in the workaday world. What is produced, for whom, with what materials, and for what purpose; how the production process is organized, administered, and divided—these are all questions about which most of us have nothing to say. I understand "oppression" to mean that our most important activities in life are determined by others and not by us ourselves.

Within this all-inclusive interference with life that is so prevalent in our working world, I do not find that men suffer any extra measure of harm or discrimination. It is women who do more work and dirtier work for less pay. Politico-economic oppression affects the great majority of people in our society whoever they are and wherever they work. The specific oppression of men, however, is a cultural matter and is most evident in the realms of leisure and the family. In these areas, too, both men and women are prevented from fulfilling their needs in very different ways, and we may want to ask if the term "oppression" is actually applicable to men in these areas.

One of the difficulties I see here is that I cannot find any obvious oppressor who is responsible for the oppression of men. Do women keep men from developing their potential? Do they keep men at a disadvantage and prevent them from fulfilling their needs? Do men themselves oppress men? Or is there some kind of conspiracy to prevent men from becoming human beings? Does society need stunted, underdeveloped men in order to function?

Keeping all these questions in mind, I would like to turn now to a concrete case. Not long ago a young woman visited me to discuss some problems she was having. She had been living together with her boyfriend for six months and she said that, except for sexual difficulties, their relationship was good. She could not reach orgasm with her partner, although she knew from masturbating that she was capable of orgasm. I asked her two questions: Do you talk together about your sex life? and Does your boyfriend even know you're having this problem? To both questions the answer was no.

I do not know either of these young people very well, but my impression of them is one of normality. They are socially adjusted and do not stand out in any particular way. That they do not speak with each other about important things strikes me as a sign of their normality. It is no doubt quite normal, too, that this young man knows nothing—or chooses not to know—and does not ask questions.

I'd like to consider this normal young man more as a type now than as a concrete case, focusing not on his particular psychic history but rather on the social conditions and attributes of his type. The adjectives that come to mind to describe him are: partially developed, crippled, limited. In the sense that these terms imply oppression, he is oppressed. He is unable to perceive and communicate. He functions well at work but only at work.

He is one of those many men who are completely out of touch with their own bodies, even if they happen to be athletic and sexually active. He is unaware of his body; the language of the body is underdeveloped in him. He does not reveal himself in movements or gestures, in blushing or turning pale. He does not dance. He has no physical ease with children. He does not bounce them on his knee, toss them in the air, let them climb all over him. He does not indulge in any spontaneous physical play with them. It would never occur to him to pretend he was a dog or a steam locomotive. To make use of an anthropological distinction: He does not live in his body. He simply *has* a body that he uses like a tool or a machine.

He always gives the impression of being without clothes even though he is dressed. You never know what he is wearing. Clothes are a medium in which the body expresses itself, and a purely functional relationship to clothes is a denial of the body on still another level. The normally oppressed man takes no pleasure in dressing up. Nor does he take pleasure in self-renewal, in self-change, in playing hide-and-seek.

It should be obvious that the many men in our culture who suffer from this kind of bodylessness did not voluntarily choose it. Just as the dolled-up female invented by the cosmetic and fashion industries is supposed to *be* nothing but body, so the male's only relationship to bodies is to *own* them, his own included. He does not live in and with his body.

It follows that this forced enmity toward the body goes hand in hand with another form of oppression—that of homosexuals. If society does not allow people to affirm their own sex, if there is either open or subtle discrimination against homosexuality, the inevitable result is the mechanization of the body that observers from the Third World find so typical of white male culture. Given this situation, the normal heterosexual becomes a victim of the oppression imposed on those who deviate from the norm. He cannot have a body because he does not allow others to be physically different from himself. Because he does not permit others to be different, he cuts off the possibility of discovering new and different possibilities in himself.

In an oppressive society, heterosexuality and antipathy toward the body are key elements in the image of the ideal man. Homosexual men often have a very different relationship to their own bodies. They walk differently; their movements are not purely task oriented. For them, the body is not just a machine that has to be oiled and refueled. It is an element of life. Many women, myself included, feel strongly attracted to homosexual men. There are no doubt many reasons for this, but one of them is probably the absence of that specifically male denial of the body.

Anyone who does not live in his body but uses it only as a machine will not be in touch with his own feelings either. That is another characteristic of the impoverished, underdeveloped male. I do not mean to say by this that men are emotionally underendowed, although it is sometimes difficult to avoid drawing this conclusion. The terrible and all too common fact is that they often have no sense of their own feelings. Fear, excitement, shame, pride, joy—all these things are present but veiled, as it were. You don't talk about them. You don't let them in and you don't let them out. This is why male emotions that do manage to find expression often seem almost funny, erupting suddenly and explosively and seeming to come from nowhere. The man who falls into a sudden fit of rage when he comes home at night is revealing how drained and humiliated his working day has left him, but he is also showing that he has never learned how to communicate his feelings, that men simply do not communicate feelings, which is why they are often so helpless if they are suddenly overwhelmed by feeling.

Just as boys, and German boys especially, learn not to cry, men learn not to deal with their feelings, not to achieve any clarity on them, not to articulate them. I know many men, intellectuals in particular, who are almost completely unable to talk about their feelings. They are emotional illiterates.

The young man we have taken as our point of departure may even know that there is something wrong in his relationship with his girl. But he has never learned how to live with his feelings. He has not developed a language that can go beyond the practical details of everyday life. Language is a machine he makes use of just as he makes use of his body. It is not a living thing, something he can work on and with in search of clarity. Women are much more likely than men to use expressions like "I don't know how to say this . . . I mean, I think . . . I can't find the right word but . . ." It never occurs to the normally oppressed man that he can't find what he wants, that there could be anything important enough to need saying here and now. Female students make excessive use of these expressions, but males seem to consider them beneath their dignity. In our sexist society, this kind of verbal hesitation is interpreted as a failing, as lack of clarity and precision, as meaningless chatter. But what this kind of searching for words actually reveals is a living relationship with language and a refusal to simply repeat what one already knows. We can imagine what a liberated society would be like in which both men and women would take part in the adventure of expanding our language, transcending language as it has come down to us.

This brings me to the third characteristic in my description of the impoverished male. He has sold out and betrayed his own desires, reducing his wishes to the same kind of mechanical banality that characterizes his movements and speech. Society has trained him not only to hide his feelings but also to cut himself off from the possibility of transcending what is. He does not dance. He does not cry. Can we imagine him praying? The idea is ludicrous.

In an early-nineteenth-century essay called "The Philistine Before, In, and After History," Clemens Brentano says of this prototype of the oppressed male that he has never felt the desire to be a tightrope walker. "No Philistine can believe that he is a Philistine. All he is capable of is being, not believing." The women's movement has revived interest in the Romantic critique of role stereotypes and of bourgeois prescriptions for male behavior. The Romantics realized very clearly that the struggle for the emancipation of women would necessarily include a struggle on behalf of impoverished and crippled men. And today, too, women do not want just an equal share of the pie as it is. They realize that they will have to bake an altogether different pie. Even in its zaniest manifestations, then, the women's movement is seeking to transcend currently enforced prescriptions of what is desirable. And it is precisely this unshackling of wishes and aspirations that the normal oppressed male finds so threatening.

The role stereotypes that are harmful to women in quite a different way deprive the male of the possibility of further self-development so that he—as in the case I mentioned at the beginning—becomes incapable of language, attentiveness, tenderness, and the ability to transcend himself in his wishes. In his behavior, he forbids his girlfriend everything that he lacks. He wants to see her in a role that is complementary to his own: He denies his body and uses his mind as an instrument, and she in turn is expected to deny her mind and use her body as an instrument. The rationally impoverished woman complements the emotionally illiterate man.

Our culture could be described as one of technocratic machismo. Machismo is an untranslatable Spanish word denoting the culture of the hypermasculine man whose relationships with women are based on feelings of male superiority, on domination and submission. The macho ideal, developed in Catholic countries, guarantees the absolute superiority of the son over the daughter, the sexual freedom of men in their relations with women, and the irresponsibility of the male toward his children.

Not long ago I came across an Italian children's book that was designed to explain sex to small children. This brochure, published by the Italian Communist Party, showed in pictures the development of life in plants, animals, and humans. I found it excellent except in one respect. When Pietro and Maria marry, they await the birth not of a child but of a son; and indeed the desired son then appears on cue. What will a boy whose mother shows him this picture book think? That he was expected and loved and his sister simply tolerated? What effects will this unconscious machismo have on him? And what is the result if this machismo merges with the Protestant work ethic to form a new cultural model? We then have a severely limited role available for the men in our society. The best, the most masculine man is the orthodox heterosexual who is raised to dominate and to take. He does not sing; he does not stammer. His need for order and dominance has long since destroyed any needs he may have felt for creativity and union with others. He is capable of work, and Freud would no doubt pronounce him capable of love, too, provided he is not impotent. But we cannot accurately describe the things that he does and experiences with the old-fashioned words "work" and "love." He cannot understand why the woman at his side is unhappy. His machismo keeps him from even imagining that it could be his fault. His oppression takes the form of impoverishment; it is the loss of his rich human potentialities.

There is perhaps no area in which we take the impoverishment of men so much for granted as in religion. They are, beyond any shadow of a doubt, irreligious and cut off from crucial human experience. Church is for women. The oppressed man of our culture does not pray. Here, too, he has lost the capacity of expressive speech. He has betrayed the dream and the hope of that land where the lion will lie down with the lamb. Dreams like that have no place in his world. Men raised in a Protestant culture find the Catholic priest's robes womanly. The prescribed irreligiosity makes it impossible for him to form any relationship to Christ, perhaps because there is in Christ too much of everything that he denies in himself. Most artists have given Jesus some feminine features. Not wanting to portray as merely masculine this human being who reflects the image of God so clearly, they have moved toward the myth of androgyny, uniting features of both sexes in their renderings.

I do not know whether Jesus was a feminist, but there is no doubt in my mind that he would be one today and would oppose the cult of the masculine.

Is there a conspiracy aimed at thwarting men's attempts to become human beings? I suspect it is the same conspiracy that indoctrinates us all in the ideology of "bigger, better, faster." The cultural impoverishment of men—and in this all men are similar whether they are blue-collar or white-collar workers—is one of the premises essential to the functioning of our social and economic system. And seen in this context, it is only logical that philosophy and poetry, music and the visual arts are being squeezed out of our schools.

Are there any signs that men will liberate themselves from this self-imposed immaturity and impoverishment? I am skeptical of any hopes that foresee a cultural liberation taking place apart from a political and economic one. But that does not mean that we should not be doing battle on the cultural front right now. Men will have to take charge of their liberation themselves. They will have to open their eyes and learn to see through the stereotypes that have deceived them into thinking their behavior was natural or masculine. It is a hopeful sign that men's groups, modeled on the consciousness-raising groups of the women's movement, have formed in the United States, that the men in them are beginning to analyze their personal experiences and histories in a political context, and that new life-styles are evolving in which the roles traditionally assigned to the sexes are changing radically.

I want to conclude with a few personal remarks. The fear I have of becoming personal and the fact that I feel obliged to apologize for doing so are, of course, also consequences of our oppressive legacy.

When I was expecting my fourth child, a feminist friend wished for me that I would have a girl. After two daughters, I was hoping for another boy, and the irritation I felt at my friend's wish prompted me to do some reflecting.

Now I am glad that I did in fact have another daughter. The task of raising my own children in society yet against it, in the world yet not of the world, as the Bible puts it, has always left me confused. Perhaps I can formulate what I feel to be most important in a child's education this way: How can one convey to a child an unshakable sense of human dignity? How can one teach a child to be proud to be a human being? How can one see to it that one's children learn to love life in such a way that they will praise it, create it, and protect it?

Faced with these questions, I find it a little bit easier to raise daughters than sons. My daughters will probably have experiences like the ones I have had. They will be put at a disadvantage, passed over, not taken seriously. As journalists, for example, they will continue to be permitted to write for the women's page. But these immediate, palpable experiences of oppression generate a positive force that joins us together with others who are experiencing far worse oppression and who, like us, are hoping and working for liberation. The dangers my son is exposed to are more difficult to combat because they go hand in hand with social recognition, success, and other bribes. In this respect, it is more difficult for him to become a human being.

My youngest daughter, who is six, recently wrote a prayer. The last two lines of it are:

> And I hope the lord is happy
> and the people are happy too.

Under the text, she painted a picture of God, a figure dancing with outspread arms. On the figure's blue dress was the word "God." God was a woman, and she was dancing. The liberated man, when he eventually appears, will be able to love this God.

6
CHRISTIANITY
AND INTOLERANCE

In the history of Christianity, the idea and the practice of tolerance have had to overcome determined resistance, and widespread acceptance of them has come slowly. In the context of general religious history, Christianity has had a conspicuous place among those religions which have proscribed and persecuted what they judged to be deviant religious behavior. This is true in a double sense, for Christianity has refused to tolerate other religious creeds and grant their adherents equal rights, and it has not been able to firmly establish the principle of religious freedom within Christian churches or to tolerate unorthodox manifestations of faith.

Massive intolerance toward other groups became historically significant after Constantine recognized Christianity as a lawful religion. Before Constantine, the church father

Tertullian had advocated the principle of religious freedom against the persecution of the pagan state, arguing that it was a basic human right to honor what one believed and to oppose official religion in the fight for one's own religion. But, as often happens in history, once those who were oppressed emerged victorious they began to see things differently; and a process of depriving pagans of their rights began, accompanied by persecution of heretics in the Christian ranks. Increasing repression was exercised against heretics who deviated from certain doctrines of faith as well as against schismatics who, in matters of discipline, saw things differently from the church. Augustine, using the Bible as his authority, provided a theological justification for the persecution of heretics and was the first to call for their physical punishment. In the fourth century, the state assumed responsibility for such punishment and incorporated it into the legal system. Islands of tolerance continued to exist in a few Arian states. For example, Theodoric the Great, a king of the Goths, declared, "We cannot dictate religion because no one can be forced to believe against his will." But by and large, Christianity's rise to power brought with it an era of new and massive intolerance. The measure of religious tolerance—along with social, political, and sexual tolerance—that the ancient world had developed was destroyed.

Destroyed by Christianity, by the religion of love. Destroyed by a religion whose founder had suffered, in his own flesh, from the intolerance of the ruling powers, a founder who had consorted with morally suspect women and chosen as a model of human mercy a Samaritan, an adherent of a false doctrine. The poor man from Nazareth was invested with the Roman emperors' symbols of power. The brother of the downtrodden became the backer of the ruling classes. We can see how this change came about from a Bible passage that played a crucial role in the growth of institutionalized intolerance and that was often cited to justify the Inquisition. The Letter of Paul to Titus says: "As for a man who is factious, after admonishing him once or twice, have nothing more to do with him, knowing that such a person is perverted and sinful; he is self-condemned" (Titus 3:10–11). This instruction reflects an early stage of debate in the early church. Sinners should be avoided; they cut themselves off from salvation because of their false understanding of faith. Thomas Aquinas cited this passage in the Bible to justify the death penalty in the law pertaining to heretics. The heretic could best be "avoided" if he was executed. From the time of the great Catharistic movement in the Middle Ages on, this kind of repressive intolerance became firmly established in the church.

The Reformation brought no significant change. Now, however, the justification offered for the punishment of heretics was not that they had to be punished for their lack of faith but that they led others astray, incited rebellion, or were blasphemous. The concept of blasphemy was applied indiscriminately, and even minor deviations from pure doctrine were included under it. Luther went so far as to call rejection of the pastoral office blasphemy. The state required strict allegiance to Reformation doctrine, and anything that departed from that doctrine was seditious.

Protestant sects and outsiders with a humanistic orientation were the first to promote a concept of tolerance. Most of the Baptists and the other leftist groups in the Reformation took freedom of religion as a basic tenet and rejected any kind of state interference in matters of faith. The humanists' defense of their new principles went something like this: "Faith cannot be coerced. Free investigation leads to the truth. Persecution is a violation of Christian love. A Christian's moral behavior is more important than strict adherence to doctrine. In the last analysis, only a few basic articles of Christian faith are important, and everyone should be free to decide other issues for him or herself, particularly since we cannot achieve certainty in any speculative matters concerning faith."

Another important way station in the bourgeois development of tolerance falls in the great religious epoch in England in the seventeenth century. In Milton, for example, we see both intellectual freedom and profound Christianity combined. For him, any coercion of faith was a sin. These Christian—not clerical—beginnings of the modern concept of tolerance were later picked up in the German Enlightenment by figures like Lessing. The Enlightenment, with its new tools of mass education such as weekly magazines, encyclopedias, and new pedagogical methods, made it a generally accepted principle that intolerance was harmful and incompatible with human dignity, that the ability to tolerate other opinions in public as well as in private life was an essential precondition for the education of the human race. Tolerance was a new value that the rising bourgeoisie successfully opposed to clerical and feudal arbitrariness.

The French constitution of September 3, 1791, contains these sentences: "Just as it guarantees natural and civil rights, the constitution guarantees to everyone the freedom to express his ideas, to write, to print, and to publish . . . and to engage in the practices of the religious sect to which he belongs. . . . Citizens have the right to elect or search out the leaders of their sects." The tolerance called for in these sentences from the French Revolutionary period assumes power and meaning because it is partisan and not merely formal in nature. It speaks out for those who, up to this time, could not speak, or write, or print, and could not choose their religious sect. It speaks out against the landholders, the aristocracy, and the clergy, which is to say that it speaks out against the oppressors. In the historical situation of those times, tolerance was a provocative and revolutionary concept. It flew in the face of the status quo, took the side of the victimized, and demanded greater freedom.

This provocative and productive concept has, with great difficulty, won out against the churches; and, on the theoretical level at any rate, we can regard its triumph as complete and final. Even the Catholic Church yields to it, though in doing so the church distinguishes between different kinds of tolerance. In theological and dogmatic issues, the Catholic Church remains as intolerant as ever because, in matters of faith, Catholicism's absolute claim to being the one true church has to be upheld. The second kind of tolerance, however, the practical middle-class type, is regarded as an obligation of Christian charity. The third kind —civil and political tolerance—has to be judged in the context of various situations. These distinctions between different kinds of tolerance suggest perhaps that we have arrived at the end of a long history of Christian intolerance, that the church has retreated to a limited position that it can hold. New, nonreligious institutions have, in the meantime, taken over the business of the Inquisition and are punishing deviations from pure political doctrine with far more effective methods—brainwashing, incarceration in mental hospitals, new methods of torture.

Has the church, then, after its long, devious detours, finally come to its senses and rid itself of its old intolerance? Or has it simply lost the power to behave with the same intolerance it displayed for so many centuries? Is not intolerance inherent in the nature of any faith that claims it is the only path to salvation? Is not intolerance not only a historical fact but also a structural characteristic of the Christian religion?

This question can be answered on a number of levels, one being the level of the sociology of religion, another that of theology. Consider for a moment, from a sociological point of view, the nature of religious groups and their attitude toward tolerance. Religious groups are normative, value-oriented groups. They lay claim to absolute and universal validity for their theological propositions. They know what is good and what is evil, what is necessary and what is superfluous for human beings. Because of this claim to universal validity, their knowledge is imperative and authoritative in character. Consequently, their communication with other groups is severely limited. "The more total the claim to validity is with which a group presents its convictions, the more obstacles the group will encounter when it tries to communicate those convictions" (G. Bormann, *Theorie und Praxis kirchlicher Organisation*, p. 173). That means that in a modern, pluralistic society, any group with a claim to universal validity will have the greatest difficulty in even making itself understood. "It becomes clear, then, that normative ideas cannot be separated from voluntative and emotional components and reduced to the cognitive level" (ibid.).

Tolerance toward others who think differently can be practiced by such groups only if they are willing to relativize and particularize their own statements. In other words, they have to admit that their purportedly absolute statements derive from a specific world view, namely, their own. In other words, they would have to limit the validity of their statements. I'd like to illustrate this point in terms of a current issue. Not long ago both the Catholic and Protestant churches in West Germany issued a joint statement on the question of abortion. This statement fell far short of the position that had been worked out in innumerable meetings beforehand, and the solution of permitting abortion in the first trimester of pregnancy was finally rejected. I do not want to discuss the issue itself here but rather give an example of intolerance in the sense of the churches' inability to place their statements in relation to the rest of society. With what right can the churches make their view binding for a large number of people who in no way share the Christian world view? With what right do they try to influence legislation instead of formulating clear guidelines for Christians, an action that would do far more to enhance their credibility? If the churches did not have to insist on implementing legal measures to enforce their world view, they would have all the more right to present moral arguments—to argue in relation to their own system of values. They could then say to a young man, as the churches of peace have been saying for centuries: As a Christian, you cannot be a soldier. And they could say to a young woman: As a Christian, you cannot get an abortion.

A time may come when this kind of political tolerance will be practiced. Indeed, there is a strong basis for it within the theological tradition.

If we look at this issue theologically—that is, within the context of assumptions that Christians take as given—we see a number of themes in the Gospels that point toward tolerance. The first of these I would call the ability of human beings to perceive. Jesus' behavior is not guided by ideas, rules, or customs but by concrete human needs. A person who sees others with an unprejudiced eye develops the ability to find alternatives. He sees, for example, that there have to be different ways to achieve the same end. He gains a critical distance on his own behavior, a distance that is essential to tolerance. This brings me to a second key element that we find exemplified in the Bible: taking into account one's own limitations, one's own possible error and possible guilt. If we learn to see ourselves as capable of error and guilt, we will learn to tolerate the erroneous thinking and, within certain limits, the erroneous behavior of others. Doubt and the capacity to criticize ourselves are the premises of true tolerance. If we feel with absolute certainty that our position is the only correct one, then the only choice that others have is to accept the revealed truth as we see it or subject themselves to it. The figures of the Bible are far removed from this kind of self-certainty. The third characteristic of Christian tolerance is patience, the abiding and enduring, as the Bible calls it, the ability to wait for change without giving up hope that change will come.

It is obvious that there are many theological concepts and attitudes that have made this kind of tolerance either impossible or, at the least, difficult to achieve. The idea of revelation, which is exclusive in nature, destroys our capacity to perceive other people. The idea of the Bible as the only source of knowledge prevents us from taking our own limitations into account.

A genuine understanding of inherent human sinfulness urges on us a productive tolerance of others.

The theological concept of tolerance has, however, very clear and definite limits, and this brings me to a theological critique of tolerance. The limits of tolerance are made manifest by the victims of a society. Wherever human beings are crippled, deprived of their dignity, destroyed, raped, that is where tolerance ends. My feeling is that today tolerance is not threatened so much by totalitarian self-certainty as it is by an all-encompassing skepticism. It is not the clergyman who is the enemy of tolerance today but the manager who is tolerant cause he thinks the truth cannot be determined. Tolerance today means room for everyone and everything, noninterference, the free interplay of forces. The provocative power that this concept had at the time it asserted itself in early bourgeois society has long since faded. My sense is that the early bourgeoisie's political demand for tolerance has its equivalent today in the proletarian demand for participation in decision making or, more clearly still, in its demand for self-determination. The repetition of the old demand therefore does not do justice to the real struggles going on today and only diverts attention from them.

The skeptical tolerance that most people adhere to these days and have internalized as a value is essentially passive and permissive. Don't get involved; it doesn't concern you. Those are two of the most important principles that bourgeois parents instill in their children, principles supported by a degenerate, worn-down understanding of tolerance. The resigned, exhausted, and inactive practitioners of this kind of tolerance may not kill anyone themselves, but they allow the killing of others to go on. They do not stand up for anyone or anything. They practice tolerance because they do not think human beings are capable of perceiving the truth. Their perpetual excuse is that we do not know enough to take sides. We supposedly did not know enough to comprehend what happened to the population of My Lai. We supposedly lack sufficient information to know for sure whether or not certain Indian tribes in Brazil were eradicated to make way for land speculators. Skeptical tolerance toward the war in Vietnam went on the assumption that the situation there was terribly complicated and difficult to understand and therefore should simply be accepted. The belief that human beings are incapable of finding the truth —or, rather, the inability to believe that they are capable of truth—destroys genuine, militant tolerance and produces a kind of London Hyde Park tolerance that lets anyone say anything but prevents everyone from acting and effecting change. It is inherent in the structure of this kind of tolerance that it is never acted on.

Despair of the truth leads to despair of—or inability to believe in—justice: We never have had justice, and we never will have it. Justice is nothing but a harebrained, foolish concept left over from prehistoric religious impulses. Tolerance conceived of this way is a far cry from the early-bourgeois provocative attitude it once was. It is instead a late-bourgeois attitude of resignation that could not be at a farther remove from Christian faith. Christ did not describe the world as a kind of Hyde Park but as a scene of human struggle and suffering. "Do not think that I have come to bring peace on earth; I have not come to bring peace, but a sword. For I have come to set a man against his father, and a daughter against her mother, and a daughter-in-law against her mother-in-law" (Matt. 10: 34–35).

Militant figures are the originators of all political and religious movements. By militant figures I do not mean the fanaticized political and religious hordes that we find cropping up in all times and in all places. What I have in mind are those historical figures and moments that make liberation immediately visible. The "intolerance" people show in those productive periods stems from their belief that the world can be comprehended and can therefore be changed and reshaped. These are periods of basic trust, not trust in the meaning of the world as it is but in the meaning that can be created in it. People in such times are capable of searching out practical truth and transforming it into reality. Because they run up against the power of the given, the massive and immovable weight of the present, they have to struggle to achieve their goals. To fight, to be intolerant in the face of what is, means to believe that there is a point in pursuing a goal and that it is possible to find meaning. Active intolerance is another indication that we respect the dignity of human beings; for we who fight have not given up on our opponent; we want to continue the association, and we believe in our opponent's future.

Theologically, the question of tolerance and intolerance cannot be separated from the question of what it is we can tolerate. Is tolerance for something like the Vietnam War possible? How can we tolerate and put up with what happened there? What meaning does a call for tolerance have in a world in which there is not just one Vietnam? What is the objective, political function of a call for tolerance in a world that, in many crucial structural respects, is dominated by a few multinational concerns?

Christian faith cannot make its peace with a kind of Hyde Park tolerance. Christianity is, by nature, militant. We cannot cease comparing this our reality with the kingdom of God. Human beings are capable of seeing the truth; they have been told what is good and what is evil; they can create justice. Truth, justice, and love are central values in the Judeo-Christian understanding of the world. Total skepticism destroys our belief that the truth can be found; it destroys, too, our thirst for justice and our yearning to live in a world ruled by love and not by the maximization of profits. Hegel called this total skepticism the "despair of reason." The demand for tolerance is, in our time, often nothing more than a disguise that this despair wears, a kind of impotent friendliness developed in reaction to the experience that in a pluralistic society different ideas and truths are at odds with each other and neutralize each other. Hegel wrote 150 years ago: "They are as badly off as Pilate, the Roman proconsul, who, on hearing Christ use the word 'truth,' responds with the question, 'What is truth?' He asks this question as a man who has no further use for such words and knows that the truth cannot be ascertained. Thus, what has always been regarded as the most shameful and most unworthy thing we can do, namely, to renounce the recognition of truth, has been elevated by our time to the highest triumph of the mind."

Perhaps our despair of reason is even greater than the one Hegel attacks here. Perhaps our skepticism toward the truth that seeks to manifest itself in concrete ways and that cannot do so without our help has grown even more. But faith and this kind of skepticism are mutually exclusive.

Hegel is, although many Christians would contest this statement, an eminently Christian thinker. A central motif in his work is "the courage to demand the truth." Early bourgeois tolerance was motivated by this courage. "Sire, give us freedom of thought!" Tolerance was demanded for the bourgeois masses in schoolrooms and universities, in editorial offices, and finally in parliaments. But it was the background of Enlightenment optimism, which maintained that the truth could be discovered and realized in the world, that gave this tolerance its significance. And this kind of optimism is at the heart of our Christian legacy: The truth asks that we recognize it and live it. This view is the very lifeblood of productive tolerance, and it is a view that excludes the tolerance of injustice. That the majority could tolerate the genocide in Vietnam was enough to make one's flesh creep. Since we are not directly confronted with the victims, there are no limits to our tolerance. Wars have always been dreadful, and injustices are committed by both sides. These are the words we use today to articulate our incapacity to believe, to hope, and to love. By contrast, faith sides militantly with the victims. Subscribing to Christian values, our faith that we are capable—and are becoming increasingly more capable—of truth, justice, and love produces a certain intolerance in us. The Christian tradition gives the name of hell to that condition in which people have cut themselves off from the essential manifestations of their communal existence. It is useless if the inhabitants of our modern hell practice tolerance as far as the temperature or the furnishings go. Christian faith seeks to realize a heaven that gives everything to everyone. If we love heaven, we find ourselves less and less able to tolerate hell.

7
UPRISING
AND RESURRECTION

Rising, uprising, and resurrection belong together factually as well as linguistically. Rising is a word that describes what an individual does in the morning; uprising, what a people does when it shakes off political sleep. Both of them mean learning how to walk upright, in a way that is still perhaps unfamiliar. To rise up means not to cringe anymore, to lose fear. A pieceworker in an electronics factory told how she used to cringe and duck down whenever the foreman came up on her from behind. Later, this became a reflex that could be set in motion by any sound reminiscent of the foreman's approach. She fell ill, torn between walking upright and cringing. No uprising took place. Under such conditions can there even be such a thing as resurrection?

We rise from sleep; we are resurrected from death. An

uprising is a rising from political sleep, from a kind of death in which people are deprived of crucial elements of their lives and are commandeered by others. It is not they themselves but someone else who determines what they produce by their work. Whether they make toys or parts for electronically guided weapons and whether what they make is sent to the Third World to maintain an oppressive order there—these questions do not lie in the competence of the people who actually produce goods. Those people do not participate in defining the purpose of their work or in organizing it. They have no say in the distribution of the goods they produce; they do not share in the profits from them. The transferring of these and other aspects of power into the hands of everyone and out of the hands of a few who represent the interests of very few—that would amount to an uprising.

Ever since Luther's time, ever since his fear of riots and unrest, words like "uprising" and "rebellion" have had a negative quality for us. We can put up with rebellions of conscience, especially if they are twenty-five years in the past. But a rebellion on the part of schoolchildren, apprentices, workers—that evokes fear.

Things are much simpler with the word "resurrection." It does not evoke anything at all, neither the fear that it perhaps inspired among Christians of the medieval period, who feared the judgment that would follow on it, nor the protests of a militant atheism such as the nineteenth century experienced. "Resurrection" does not even evoke ridicule. There are words that are so dead now, so utterly lost to usage, that their only function is to remind us that the language we live in is a kind of prison. Heidegger has called language the "house of existence." If there is no word for something, it does not exist. But this statement may not be quite concrete enough, and we have to realize that the language we use and that determines our behavior is a prison too, one that prevents our thinking and wishing from being truly free, a prison with cells and workrooms and regularly scheduled exercise periods in the courtyard. The word "resurrection" has been excluded from that exercise yard where words like "horse" and "fountain" still find a place. These words may, of course, eventually suffer the same fate as resurrection. Then we will hear tell of such things only in the language of fairy tales and dreams, just as now we sometimes hear tell of resurrection in the language of poetry.

> I sing for my Comrade Dagobert Biermann
> who became smoke from the chimneys
> and is risen stinking from Auschwitz
> into the often-changing heavens of this earth
> and whose ashes are strewn for eternity
> over all the seas and among all peoples.

This is one way that we can in fact talk about resurrection these days, for if we say that Christ is risen but do not dare to say that Dagobert Biermann is risen, then the first statement becomes meaningless. We cannot believe in resurrection for some but not for others. It is an all-inclusive symbol of life for everyone, a kind of life that gives meaning to death. No one has died in vain. This is the claim that resurrection throws in the face of death. As in the Bible, of course, so here in Wolf Biermann's poem, witnesses are essential to resurrection, people who pass on to others what they have seen. The Romans, in their day, had their fun with the fact that there were no nonbelievers among the witnesses of the resurrection, no educated skeptics of, say, Pilate's sort. But that is perfectly logical, difficult as it may be for a Roman head to comprehend. For a Roman mind, the resurrection is either a fact that can be photographed, or it is a religious hallucination. From this point of view, a mortal human is an individual being, a subject of the law, and, perhaps, a personality who is guaranteed continuing existence in the resurrection. If we confine ourselves to thinking of a human being as a creature existing in isolation, then it is difficult to conceive of the resurrection as meaning anything. We remain trapped in the prison of language; our consciousness can go only as far as the possibilities of our language will let it. Transcendence has become meaningless and socially ridiculous, and all human wishes that go beyond what exists here and now and beyond what is visible have been destroyed. The dead are indeed dead, and the implication of that statement is that the living are simply the not-yet-dead. But for Wolf Biermann, the dead are not simply beings that can no longer fulfill their functions in bourgeois society, functions like buying and selling, having and being had. In his view, the living and the dead have a different relationship to each other; they have a common history called "The Revolution Betrayed," and that is the subject of Biermann's poem. They also have a common name, "Comrade," that evokes this common history, a history in which the dead are not excluded. Then, too, they have a common future, the living and the dead; and that is why this poem goes on to say more about Dagobert Biermann, "who is risen stinking from Auschwitz . . .

> and who is murdered again every day
> and who rises again every day in the struggle
> and who is risen with his comrades
> in my smoky song.

I hope Wolf Biermann will forgive me if I say—in my language—that this poem is about Christ, who was murdered in Auschwitz and in Vietnam and in all the other continuations of Auschwitz we have witnessed. It is about Christ, who will remain in the fear of death until the end of the world and who will rise from the dead wherever people carry on and fight in the cause he began. Christ, who needs Wolf Biermann's song as much as we do. The liturgy is meant as much for the dead as for the living, and those who have no graves are in special need of Biermann's smoky song.

Uprising and resurrection belong together here. Biermann's poem ends with the words: "In unbroken humility I sing rebellion." Without the resurrection of the dead, this rebellion would be incomplete, and resurrection without any rebellion—but I do not want to talk anymore about that. Resurrection without rebellion has been preached so persistently for two thousand years that there is almost nothing left of the truth that the man who was executed on Golgotha showed us. Today, it is essential that we see the mythical figures of rebellion and resurrection, Prometheus and Christ, as one. Marx called Prometheus the greatest saint in the calendar, Prometheus the rebel, who stole fire from the gods to give it to the human race. We have fallen into the habit of seeing Prometheus as the opposite of Christ. But if we look more carefully at his fate as myth has handed it down to us, we are struck by the structural similarities in the stories of these two figures and between the figures themselves.

Hesiod relates how Prometheus, acting as an arbiter in a dispute between humans and the gods over who should get the larger portion of sacrificial animals, decided in favor of the humans. That is much like Jesus' reclaiming of the Sabbath—the sacrifice the Jewish world made to God —for men. Humanity does not exist for the sake of the Sabbath, he taught, but the Sabbath for the sake of humanity. Prometheus felt no fear of Zeus and honored humans instead. He "reduced the omnipotence of the immortals," we are told. Jesus was condemned, too, for doing things that were reserved to God alone: He forgave sins, healed the sick, raised the dead. Prometheus prevented Zeus from destroying humankind. He gave human beings fire and insight into the order of the world, taught them mathematics and technology. His punishment for siding with humans is to suffer. He is rendered powerless, taken to a desolate place where no one can hear him or be heard by him. With nails and chains he is pinned down so he cannot move, hung in an unnatural posture, hated by the gods and abandoned by men. In his tragedy of Prometheus, Aeschylus describes how, at the beginning of this process that we can call "crucifixion," the condemned Prometheus remains silent under torture. The final words of the play are: "You see what injustice I suffer." *Paschō*, I suffer—the same word as in ·Christ's passion. Prometheus was—and these are Aeschylus' actual words—full of mercy but experienced no mercy himself; he freed humankind but could not free himself; he was a physician but could find no cure for himself. Aeschylus' explanation of why Prometheus had to suffer is perfectly clear: He was bound, hung in chains, and abandoned "because he loved humankind too much." If we try to summarize the reasons for Jesus' death on the cross, we find ourselves using very similar formulations: He helped others, but he could not help himself; he loved "too much." But however powerless Prometheus is, he is more powerful than the tyrant Zeus and he will overcome him. He has shown the way to a new, more humane world, and it is for this very act that he must pay the price of extreme suffering. Christians, too, believe that there is no resurrection without pain and suffering and the death of those whom Wolf Biermann calls the betrayed comrades. The price we have to pay for a truly human life has not become less since ancient times, much as we may want to believe that it has. People are still being tortured today because they have fought for justice. People are still dying today from the indifference of others who do not want rebellion and do not need resurrection. But despite the betrayal of the revolution and, God knows, the betrayal of Christ, we see happening again and again what we all need most: uprisings of life against the many forms of death; which is to say, resurrection.

II
FOUNDATIONS
OF A FEMINIST
THEOLOGY

8
MYSTICISM—LIBERATION— FEMINISM*

Dear friends! I would like to present here my own preliminary ideas on mysticism and feminism, my own questions, with the understanding that this is a rough draft, as it were, and not a finished and polished lecture. The explanation for this has to do with the difficulty of the subject and with the fact that our thinking on this problem is still in its early stages. We just do not have a feminist description of mystical theology. We have instead descriptions written by men about phenomena colored by quite specific circumstances, and this makes it difficult to achieve

*This talk was presented on June 19, 1980, in Hamburg, Germany, under the auspices of the Evangelische Akademie Nordelbien. It was subsequently published in *Orientierung. Berichte und Analysen aus der Arbeit der Evangelischen Akademie Nordelbien*, No. 3, July–September 1980, pp. 44–61.

any clarity about this immense topic of mysticism and its links to feminism and liberation.

Perhaps you may be wondering what these imposing substantives "feminism," "liberation," and "mysticism" have to do with each other at all. What is their common denominator? We can say that there are people who are involved in the search for nonauthoritarian human relationships and who are working toward the abolition of class rule and class injustice. That is what the word "liberation" suggests here. They are also working to abolish patriarchy and the colonialization of women (I will explain more exactly a little later what I mean by this), and they are searching for a nonauthoritarian language to use in describing a God whose essential attributes are not independence, distance, power, and domination. In other words, the search for nonauthoritarian relationships and conditions is, as I see it, what unites feminists, mystics, and advocates of liberation.

I would like to attempt some definitions of the three concepts in question. Going on what I have learned from the liberation theology of Latin America, I feel it is crucial to stress the multidimensionality of liberation in any definition we give of it. It is essential to understand that in speaking of liberation we are talking about something that affects our economic, political, and social life and our psychological, cultural, and religious life. Partial liberation or the idea that we will be liberated if there is a change in governments and another clique comes to power is not liberation in the broad sense I mean here.

One of the most powerful symbols of liberation in theology is Israel's escape from Egypt in the Exodus. Exodus is both a story and an interpretation of a story in which various aspects of human life are addressed under the concept of "liberation." In Exodus, we learn of slaves who were forced to make twice as many bricks as they had been making. That is an example of economic oppression. We see a people that had lost its national identity free itself with the help of its national leader, Moses. We see a people that was not allowed to sing its songs or worship as it pleased, a people that had lost its cultural identity and that became free in leaving Egypt. And the freedom it won was this multidimensional freedom.

Those of us who plead for the economic and social liberation of oppressed peoples are often criticized for limiting our concern to the economic sector, but I feel such criticism is reductive and therefore inept. Our concern is not limited to economics alone. Economics and psychology cannot be considered separately, and religion, too, is affected by socioeconomic conditions. Although the Israelites were materially better off in Egypt than they were in the desert, they could not praise, glorify, and honor God the way they wanted to as long as they remained slaves. Religious liberation for them meant not a turning away from God but rather a turning toward him. How can we sing the Lord's praises in an alien land? How can we praise God in a system of structuralized injustice, in a society based on exploitation? That is the question that comes to my mind in this connection.

Liberation is multidimensional, and we will be able to understand the concept of liberation in its historical profundity only if we understand it in its different dimensions. Another story I would like to tell here, along with the Exodus story, is one about a woman in Nicaragua who was interviewed by journalists a few months ago as she stood in front of a school that had just been built in a rural province there. She was a very old woman, seventy-two years old, and one of the journalists asked her, "Can you read?" Her response was, "Not yet." I find this a wonderful story about liberation, for it contains the various dimensions I have in mind when I think about liberation, a major dimension being that of an economy which is not geared to the increase of profits alone. Why, after all, should anyone teach a seventy-two-year-old woman to read? That won't raise the gross national product one whit. This woman had developed a new consciousness that she expressed in her brief reply. She felt new hope. Her psychological state had been altered by the revolution. Her religious state may be altered by the revolution, too, in the sense that the hope of living a decent human life may awaken in her again. So much for liberation.

Turning briefly to feminism now, I understand under feminism that segment of the women's movement which fights not only for the equality of women but also for a different culture. A distinction has to be made between this women's movement and an earlier one, the bourgeois women's movement, whose major concern was to win equal rights and opportunities for women. For example: "Women musicians in the Berlin Philharmonic"—that would be nice. Or "German faculties of theology employ women professors"—that would be very nice too. "Women participate in the Salt II disarmament talks." We could go on to name many more examples. I mention these to indicate how important it is that women have a part in all these things, in our cultural and political life.

But at the same time I'd like to point out that this effort is not enough and that a feminist position has to go beyond it. As American feminists like to say, the point is not to become a vice-president at General Motors. The point is to change General Motors so radically that neither it nor we will need any more presidents or vice-presidents. What we need is another culture with goals and values different from the ones currently in force. The essence of feminism is not just a big "Me, too!" It is the creation of something new. We do not want to become like men and have and do everything that they have and do. We want a different kind of life; that is feminism in its most profound form today, and this is what I mean when I say that it is the conscious segment of the women's movement that wants this cultural change and is working to effect it.

I feel I have to pause here briefly to anticipate some misunderstandings that often crop up in this context. These feminists are not assuming that women are all better than men and that everything would be better if women finally got their chance to come to power. No one gives serious consideration to this kind of talk. These are simply lies disseminated by a ruling patriarchy that has not the slightest idea what feminism really is.

I think, however, that it is important to realize how the dominant culture restricts our language and our capacity for speech. I would like to illustrate this with some examples from a field I am familiar with, namely, theology. The repression of women is perhaps more glaring in theology than anywhere else. The most striking example is the refusal of the Catholic Church to ordain women, and even though women can be ordained in the Protestant Church, their opportunities there are severely limited. But what I have primarily in mind here is the discipline of theology per se. I do not think that 51 percent of humanity can be kept silent without the other 49 percent suffering ill effects from that silence. I am convinced that the men who exercise this kind of power experience a loss and are in some way destroyed by their own actions. What they cut off, crush, prevent, and leave unarticulated damages them, too.

The catastrophic consequences this has for theology are obvious in theological language. I feel that the silencing of the feminine side of the soul and the subordination of everything that smacks of womanhood, the condescension that is so often in play whenever someone is described as feminine—I feel that this kind of domination and arrogance is most destructive for those who practice it. This male self-destruction has done more to destroy theology than all the attacks of the secular world combined.

In a process of purging and impoverishment, theological language has been stripped of all the holistic, emphatic, and integrative qualities we are familiar with from the Gospels. So-called "scientific" theology usually expresses itself in language void of consciousness. This language reflects no consciousness because it is empty of emotion, insensitive to human experience, ghostlike, neutral, uninteresting, unappealing, flat. It admits of no doubt, which is to say it represses the shadow side of faith and does not lift it into consciousness. All you need to do to understand what I mean is to read a few commentaries by male theologians on the story of the fall in the Bible. Then you will see how they speak about women, about Eve, who is, after all, the one who brought down all this misery upon us.

These commentaries always begin something like this: "Who would be so foolish as to talk to a snake in the first place? A woman. It was a woman who was so curious she had to talk with a snake. Nobody in his right mind would do such a thing!" That is the kind of prohibition on thought that is the rule in male theology, a prohibition on inquiry, an across-the-board condemnation of intellectual and sexual curiosity. By contrast, conscious, integrative, emphatic language is crucial to a theology that truly touches people. You cannot reach people if you are divorced from your own emotions. In scholarly and scientific language, "emotional" has become a derogatory term. When I am told, "Don't be so emotional," as I often am, all I can say in response is, "If only you were!"

A language that takes our emotions seriously and gives them real weight in our lives encourages us to think and be and act differently, but current scholarly language in theology achieves this quality of real, living speech only rarely. And when it does, it does so by way of flaws in the system, as it were, because no theologian can actually attain to the sterile heights of this antiemotional, neutralistic theology that negates human experience. If one has managed to preserve a modicum of humanity, that humanity will sometimes come sneaking through by subversive routes. This can happen if we do not let ourselves be guided solely by such questionable scholarly ideals as neutrality, disinterestedness, and the absence of emotion; if we do not join in the efforts of theology—and of other disciplines as well—to make subjective consciousness disappear.

I do not know how prevalent these attitudes are in German universities, but I have heard from young students at Harvard that the first thing they learn is not to say "I." That is forbidden. An "I" gets you a red pencil mark. You just don't say things like that. In learning the language of domination, these students learn to give up their subjectivity, their emotionality, their range of experience, their partisanship.

I'd like to make another remark now that is addressed to the men in this hall. The word "feminism" often evokes fear in men. One reason for this is that men are often totally ignorant of what feminism really is. Another reason is that feminism has been grossly misrepresented in the mass media. But there are deeper fears at work here, too. Many men assume, for example, that they cannot be feminists. This false assumption can be traced back to a misuse of language. About ten years ago an essay titled "Was Jesus a Feminist?" received considerable attention in religious circles in America. It was plain that the answer was "yes" because of Jesus' attitudes toward and treatment of women and his tearing down of hierarchical rules. I mention this only to illustrate that a man can, of course—because feminism is not a form of racism that simply excludes men—that he can and should call himself a feminist if he shares these desires for liberation, change, and a new culture. He should not be afraid of the concept of feminism. It is militant but not exclusive. That is not its point.

Women do, of course, sometimes feel a need for temporary exclusiveness, a need to separate themselves from men. One of the reasons for this is, for example, the universally recognized fact that on occasions like this one it is usually the men who are the first to ask questions, even if there are more women in the audience than men. For reasons of this kind there are women like Mary Daly (whose book *Beyond God the Father* [Beacon Press, 1973] has just appeared in German) who do not speak with men and who, in gatherings like this one, do not answer questions that men ask. I don't think that is right, and I have very different feelings about this question, although I can understand how a woman could come to that position. But I would like to emphasize that as far as I am concerned feminism is not limited to people with female reproductive organs.

And now for mysticism, which is surely the most unclear and unfathomable of all these terms. I mentioned to a non-Christian friend the subject of my talk this evening, and she said, "Oh, yes," and then added a remark that made it perfectly clear that mysticism meant nothing to her but irrationality and inane religious superstition. To say that something is mystical is about the same thing as saying—in Marxist usage—that it is pure nonsense. It is not this usage I am concerned with here but rather the experience, or that part of religious experience, that views itself as mystical.

The best definition of mysticism, the classical definition, is a *cognitio Dei experimentalis*, a perception of God through experience. This means an awareness of God gained not through books, not through the authority of religious teachings, not through the so-called priestly office but through the life experiences of human beings, experiences that are articulated and reflected upon in religious language but that first come to people in what they encounter in life, independent of the church's institutions.

Mysticism can occur, then, in all religions; and it almost always clashes head-on with the hierarchy dominant in its time. It is an experience of God, an experience of being one with God, an experience that God bestows on people. It is a call that people hear or perceive, an experience that breaks through the existing limitations of human comprehension, feeling, and reflection. This element of shattering old limitations is crucial to the mystical experience, and it is responsible for the difficulty of communicating mystical experience: It is impossible to speak about what lies beyond the capabilities of speech, yet anyone who has had mystical experience feels compelled to speak about it. The language he or she uses will therefore be paradoxical, self-contradictory, and obscure. Or it may lead to silence, for silence is one of the modes of mystical experience.

What I would like to stress here is that we should not regard mystics as people at some great remove from ourselves, nor as people with unique experiences incomprehensible to all the rest of us. One of the greatest mystics and probably the greatest German mystic, Meister Eckhart, never—as far as we are able to tell—saw visions or heard voices. He reflected on religious experience without reference to these specific visionary or auditory phenomena. The crucial point here is that in the mystical understanding of God, experience is more important than doctrine, the inner light more important than church authority, the certainty of God and communication with him more important than believing in his existence or positing his existence rationally.

Here, too, I would like to give an example, one that did not originally come under the heading of mysticism but that illustrates the broad sense in which I understand this concept. During a class at the seminary where I teach in New York, the question of religious experiences came up. An embarrassed silence followed, of course. No one in this generation will admit to such experiences or can talk about them. Finally, though, a young woman raised her hand, and a week later she reported on her religious experience. What she had to say made a profound impression on me.

She told how she used to read a great deal when she was

fourteen, especially at night, like so many of us. Her parents did not allow her to stay up late, because she was supposed to be asleep and living a well-ordered life. One night she had read in bed for several hours and then, waking suddenly at four in the morning with her head full of what she had been reading, she went out into the winter night, looked at the stars, and had—as she told it—a feeling of happiness that was unique for her, a feeling of unity with all of life, with God, an experience of overpowering clarity and joy, a sense of being cared for and borne up: No ill can befall me; I am indestructible; I am one with the All. This was the kind of language she used to describe her experience. She then went on to say that she didn't have this experience again until later in her life and in a totally different context. This other context was a major demonstration against the Vietnam War. There, too, she felt cared for, a part of the All, felt herself together with others participating in the truth of the All. For her, both these experiences belonged together under the heading "religious experience."

If this same young woman had lived in fourteenth-century Germany, she probably would have said, "I heard a voice, and it said to me, 'I am with you' "—or something like that. Or she might have said, "I saw a light." In the twentieth century, she can't use that kind of language to communicate her experiences to others. She has to struggle with the language and with her own embarrassment. We have no language at all that can describe these experiences precisely, yet she had the courage to try to tell us what she had felt. And I would guess that if you look back on your own life history, you will recall similar experiences, states of "being high," to use the banal expression, states related to mental and spiritual experiences for which religious language provides a kind of home or mode of expression.

Mystical experience is not, then, something extraordinary, requiring some special talent or sixth sense. Thousands of people in other cultures have had such experiences, experiences of this happiness, this wholeness, this sense of being at home in the world, of being at one with God. It makes no difference—and this point has been confirmed by everyone who has ever reported on mystical experience—whether these experiences are interpreted with the aid of a personal God or nontheistically, as in oriental mysticism. Whether we see these experiences in terms of the Tao or of God is not central to them. How we view them will depend on the culture we live in, our past experiences, the languages we have learned. What is appalling in our culture is that most people have no language at all for describing such experiences. And the result of that is, of course, that these experiences go uncommunicated to others, are lost and forgotten. We are unable to tell anyone else about the most important experiences we have.

If you will permit me a brief historical aside, I would like to say that one purpose I see for this lecture is to encourage people to communicate with each other about these vitally important experiences. This will enable us to keep them alive and derive productive energy from them.

I am not a historian, and I do not have enough historical knowledge to relate this whole issue to the thirteenth and fourteenth centuries in Germany. But I do think it important to realize that the women's movement has one of its precursors in the religious life of this period in Germany. There was great unrest among women who were finding they could not be content either in marriage as it was or in the cloisters as they were. Both were inadequate for a full life. Women realized that, and the spirit of unrest spread. Women touched by this spirit called themselves the "sisters of the free spirit." They became mystics, had visions, heard voices. The mothers superior, particularly those of the Dominican order, sought to channel and discipline these energies, just as the Franciscans had. This free, untamed spirit that shattered existing limitations, including institutional ones, had to be channeled, directed, and limited; but the social and historical conditions that led to the founding of these many Beguine communities, in which mysticism flourished, were an undeniable reality; and that the Beguine movement was a kind of liberation movement is a fact that has come to be admitted even in more or less orthodox Catholic interpretations. Indeed, these interpretations are ready to call the movement a kind of emancipation, though they also add that this term has to be properly understood.

But now we must ask what the connection between these three components of mysticism, liberation, and feminism is. For those of us in the feminist movement who see ourselves as Christians or as religious, mystical theology is, in my view, the greatest support the tradition can give us on the long road to liberation and emancipation.

I would like to present five theses now that will, I hope, bring these ideas together into some kind of unity. I will read these short sentences, then take them up one by one. They represent a sketch of a feminist theology. At the moment, we are in the building stages, searching and feeling our way. The classical work in this field remains to be written.

1. Theology originates in pain.
2. Faith is liberation from colonialism.
3. Feminist theology is a theology of liberation.
4. The image of God is subject to change.
5. Mysticism means learning to yield up the self completely.

Theology originates in our need for more, in our sense of failure, in our awareness of life destroyed. Its locus is suffering or the disregard for life that we experience all the time. Take one of the simplest prayers from the Christian tradition: "Create in me a clean heart, O God." The prayer arises from an experience of being dirtied, humiliated, destroyed, from a sense of life unlived. Or: "Thy kingdom come." The kingdom that is not yet here. The kingdom of justice and freedom we are all seeking. Theology originates in these experiences of negative forces. If we take this idea seriously, then theology has no business being deductive anymore, that is, based on established theological principles. It should be inductive, working from human experience.

It is meaningless, for example, to use as a point of departure for our theology statements like "Christ is the Son of God" or "In the beginning God created the heavens and the earth" or "They will sit at the right hand of the Father," and so on and so forth. This kind of deductive language is dying out in theology. We can see that this is happening, even though fundamentalist Christians are doing their best to keep such language alive. I do not think there is much we can derive from these sentences any longer. But if we take statements of a completely different sort, ones that convey human experience, such as, "Mrs. Schmidt has been waiting for seventeen months for an 8-by-12-foot room in a nursing home," we can make theology out of them. That is a better way to get hold of what really counts. I've noted still another sentence here: "The cosmetics industry was able to increase its sales in this area by 40 percent." That is an inductive theological statement, one we can draw conclusions from, one that can lead us somewhere.

Theology begins with experience and sets experience over against the promise of a whole life, the promise of the Kingdom of God. It confronts these statements with the genuine life that has been promised us, which is no more nor less than everything for all of us. And only if we engage in this kind of theology can we rediscover the language Jesus used. His language was not deductive either; he did not begin with established principles. I selected the two statements above as representative of "social conditions" to dramatize my point. But perhaps—in the light of what I said earlier about religious experiences and the possibilities for religious experience—we should add something undramatic here and mention what the banality of our repetitive, everyday lives does to us. This daily functioning—everything goes very smoothly; we get up, have breakfast, and then the day takes its usual course without anything at all happening—this kind of death by a-religious banality can also be used as a means of understanding from what sources of experience theology takes its vitality and what its tasks are. The method has to be inductive; it has to be a narrative method.

To say that the most important thing to do is to relate human experience is a new and different concept for theological methodology. Chris's story, which I just told you, what she had to say about her life at fourteen and twenty-three, is a narration, the story of one human being and her experiences. I feel we have to oppose the abracadabra of organized religion with something else. When, for instance, people say, "Jesus lives," that is in itself a nice enough statement, but how much better it would be if they added, "And with him I live, too." But as the sentence "Jesus lives" is usually used, it has very little concrete relationship to Jesus. It is an abstraction from the image of Jesus or from the dominant religious language.

Now to move on to my second statement: Faith is liberation from colonialism. Faith is, as it were, continuing exodus from Egypt. As the Jewish liturgy puts it: "You should regard yourselves as those who are departing from Egypt today." And with the Israelites, we too should continue to emigrate from this Egypt of alien domination, of insipid life, of trouble-free functioning, and of colonialism. In speaking of the oppression of women specifically, I find the word "colonialism" very appropriate. When a colonial power comes into a country—into a black country, let us say—it takes over everything of importance: schools, churches, transportation, production. All the positions of power are occupied by whites. The blacks are permitted to fill subordinate positions, but the main thing that happens is that colonialism imposes a colonial mentality on them, and they come to believe that the white father knows best.

It is easy to apply this paradigm to women. The same subordination holds sway in the minds and hearts of women. They are colonialized, which is to say they experience themselves as weak, powerless. My daughter says to me, "I can't do math," although she is highly intelligent. If she were a boy, she wouldn't talk such nonsense.

What I mean is that the destruction of women's outlook on life, as we witness that destruction in the middle class, is still a reality. Or perhaps I should say it is still a reality for my generation. Yours is clearly much farther along in this regard. The norm for women is what Betty Friedan has called the feminine mystique: the destruction of women's lives, stultifying conventions, prohibitions on thinking about anything outside the family, confinement to colonial status. These are the demands placed on women. These are the things the colonial rulers have taught them. You are not permitted to think, to develop your talents, to invest your energies wholly in anything outside the family. I am not speaking so much for you who are here in this room as I am for the thousands of our sisters outside it whose experiences have been what I have just described and who have internalized patriarchy's prohibitions on thought so completely that they don't even dare to question them. Their lives are lived on someone else's terms. They do not know what self-determination is.

I'd like to make this point somewhat clearer by explaining what part female piety has played in this complex; for piety, religion, certainly has a role in it. Of the three areas traditionally assigned to women in our culture—church, children, kitchen—it is the church that acts as a lubricant, as it were, of women's oppression. It is true, of course, that in religion some part of woman's human dignity is preserved; but I feel nonetheless that the piety the churches have offered women and that women have internalized is essentially a kind of Uncle Tom piety. "Uncle Tom" is the name the black liberation movement has given to blacks who may well be profoundly good and decent people but who love and honor the masters who enslave them and who find even the idea of rebellion inconceivable. They remain submissive, and the black power movement has therefore parted company with them, trying to explain at the same time what is wrong with Uncle Tomism and why it is of no help to anyone.

The feminist movement still has a long way to go in this area. I don't know exactly how to describe this female dilemma in appropriately feminist language, this sense of being dominated, stupefied, limited, boxed in, this feeling of "I can't do anything." I can't go for a walk at night or I'll get raped. I can't hitchhike. That's really going too far. I'd be giving the men who pick me up the wrong idea. I can't choose this or that profession. I can't put a fuse in the fuse box if the lights go out—and so on and so forth.

I'm sure you can find your own examples, and I'm also sure that every woman in this room who is honest with herself has one or two areas in which she has internalized this "I can't," this image of her helplessness that the oppressor has imposed on us. Now liberalization from colonialism begins with an awareness both of this oppression and of the possibility of self-realization, the possibility of becoming a human being, a Christian, an active force, an adult, becoming capable of love and work, of finally ridding oneself of the little girl's role, of this lovable helplessness that is part of the image the oppressor has prescribed for us.

I see feminist theology—and here I come to my third point—as a liberation theology; and under liberation theology we classify different theologies that, all working from different perspectives, such as the perspective of race, class, or sex (i.e., the perspective of being black, poor, or female) seek to establish themselves as new forms of theological consciousness.

A basic assumption of all these theologies is the interpretation of redemption, in the religious sense, to mean liberation. Redemption is not the granting of salvation to a specific individual. It is instead an occurrence that takes place in this world and for everyone of this world. It does not touch just some individuals but has instead a liberating character for all humankind. The Greek word *sōteria*, which has traditionally been translated as redemption, is now translated as liberation, salvation in the sense of liberation. Theologically, this interpretation has a certain anti-Protestant character that I would like to enlarge upon here. Protestantism has always stressed human sinfulness and our inability to change the conditions of our lives. Luther wrote: "Did we in our own strength confide, our striving would be losing." Luther's reference was, of course, to God or, more precisely, to Christ, who fights on our behalf. But these lines have in fact been interpreted and experienced throughout our social history as an admission of powerlessness. From Luther's time to Hitler and beyond, the typical German motto has been: "There's nothing we can do." We cannot change anything; with the little power we have there is nothing we can do.

In the process of Protestant socialization, this feeling of impotence, helplessness, powerlessness, this sense that there is nothing people can do to change their fate, becomes deeply internalized. What was originally meant in a purely theological context has, then, been adapted to the social and political realm, where it has had the most catastrophic possible effects on German history. This ideology of helplessness is still with us today, even though its religious character has receded far into the background. There is a late capitalistic ideology of helplessness that is constantly telling us that there is nothing we can do. We have a new arms buildup; we have new medium-range nuclear missiles; there is nothing we can do to change all that.

But if that is true, why is it that 51 percent of the Dutch voted against the stationing of these new missiles on their territory, and why hasn't the same thing happened in Germany? Why haven't we even had any genuine public debate of this issue? How can that be? I do not want to undertake a full analysis of this question now, but there is—among other reasons—a religious reason as well, namely, our internalized helplessness. God is so strong because we are so weak. The weaker and more helpless we are, the stronger and greater that makes God. The smaller we make ourselves, the larger we make him. We put all our trust in him. This kind of talk in which we belittle our own capabilities to see the truth and to act on it is similar to the belittling of women's intelligence and capabilities, and both kinds of belittlement and disparagement are standard practices throughout our society.

The decisive change in our new understanding of liberation, of the women's movement, and of feminist theology is evident in our concept of God. The ways we address God, and the symbolism of God we use, change and have to change if we take this demand for liberation seriously and try to incorporate it into our lives. This has to do with what I said before about the powerlessness that we experience and that religion glorifies and intensifies. This powerlessness destroys the strength that we have. We conceive of God as a powerful, indeed, as an all-powerful, father. There are two important components to this symbol. One is power, omnipotence. Take the *pater familias* as defined in Roman law. He had the right, for instance, to either accept or reject a baby. And if the baby happened to be a girl—which is to say, a rather superfluous object—it was very often rejected and left to perish. The father was power incarnate, lord over life and death. He was economic power, moral power, political power; and he was also the embodiment of kindness. Both these components are present in the image of God the Father, and they are what make it such an important and powerful image.

But as a woman I have to ask why it is that human beings honor a God whose most important attribute is power, whose prime need is to subjugate, whose greatest fear is equality. Just recall that awful sentence at the end of the story of the Fall when God says that if Adam and Eve continue to behave this way they'll wind up eating from the tree of life, too. So he has no choice but to throw them out of paradise quickly. He has to drive them out; otherwise, as it says in the Bible, they will become "like one of us." What kind of a God is that, whose major interests have to be described in these terms? A being who is addressed as "Lord," a being whom his theologians have to describe as all-powerful because he cannot be satisfied with being merely powerful?

The most important criticisms that an incipient feminist theology has to make of the current dominant theology are directed against these phallocratic fantasies, against the accumulation of power and the worship of power. Why should we honor and love a being that does not transcend but only reaffirms the moral level of our present male-dominated culture? Why should we honor and love this being, and what moral right do we have to do so if this being is in fact no more than an outsized man whose main ideal is to be independent and have power? If that is God's main interest—and we can cite one theology after another in which God's main interest is defined this way—then there is no reason in this world for a woman to love, honor, or respect such a being. I don't think there is any reason for a man to love, honor, or respect him either, but my focus here is the group that is most directly affected and oppressed by this being.

I'd like to illustrate this a little further in the context of my own theological autobiography, because very early on in my career I had difficulties with this dispenser of power. I was born in 1929, and these difficulties began for me in connection with the most important political event my generation had to deal with, that is, with the reality of Auschwitz. As a young theologian, I could not understand how people could talk about an almighty God after something like Auschwitz had happened. I could not bring these two things together. It simply went beyond my powers to conceive of a powerful God who could look at Auschwitz, tolerate it, participate in it, observe it, or whatever. If he is all-powerful, then he is devoid of love. Such was my conclusion.

So I proceeded to write a book titled *Ein Kapitel Theologie nach dem Tode Gottes* (A Chapter of Theology After the Death of God)—because I genuinely felt that this heavenly being did not exist anymore and that we had to take seriously the trend in philosophy (as in Nietzsche, for example) that had abolished this being and regarded him as dead. I then developed a radically Christocentric theological position, following Dietrich Bonhoeffer's lead and beginning with the powerless Christ who died on the cross, who had no legions behind him, no power that could rescue him or free him. In this theology, God himself, a God who acts and speaks, is inaccessible to us. The only guide we have is this nonauthoritarian, powerless Christ who has nothing but love, who exerts no power, has no armies to call on, shouts no one down, as God did Job out of the whirlwind, who has nothing with which to save us but his love. His powerlessness constitutes his inner authority. We are not his because he sired us, created us, made us. We are his because love is his weaponless power, and that power is stronger than death.

That was the essence of my position in the context of what was known as theology after the death of God. My difficulties with this father, creator, purveyor of power, and master of history only increased, though, as I began to understand more clearly what it meant to be born as a woman—to be born incomplete, as Freudian psychology likes to put it—and to live in a patriarchical society. My difficulties with this God arose from the historical circumstances of this century and from my national identity as a German.

But they became more profound and changed in emphasis as I became more involved with feminism. How could I want power to be the central category of my life? How could I honor a God who was not more than a man? If I just blurt out what comes automatically to my mind when I think of male power, I would mention yelling, giving orders, learning to shoot—things like that.

I do not feel that I personally have suffered much damage at the hands of patriarchy. There are others who have suffered much more. I have been harmed by it only to the extent that we have all been harmed by it. And all of us do suffer damage from this kind of colonialization that we have all experienced and that we are still experiencing. It has become increasingly clear to me that any identification whatsoever with the aggressor—that is, with someone who comes from outside me, subjugates me, and then goes on to tell me that this is just the way things should be, that this is the state preordained for me—any identification with such an aggressor is the worst disaster that can befall a woman. And it is still befalling millions. The symbol of the father does not exert the same fascination for those who will never be fathers as it does for those who will. And power tempered by mercy, the image of the kindly father, is no solution to the problem either. A kindly slaveholder may be loved and honored by his slaves, and this is the form that female piety basically takes, as I mentioned before: submission to the roles that God has ordained for women. That is the equivalent of knuckling under to a kindly, well-meaning father. But submission and obedience destroy our possibilities to become human beings, and I know from the history of my country and from the sexism of the dominant culture that a father figure cannot liberate us.

The question we have to ask theologically is: Do the word and the symbol "father" still have real meaning for us? Do they say enough if we are making a truly serious effort to say something about God?

I'd like to stop for a moment to qualify what I've just said and make clear that whenever we speak of God we speak symbolically. Symbols are the only means we have for talking about God. The problem is, however, that if a given symbol becomes dominant, the slightest doubts or questionings of that symbol can evoke defensive reactions that are out of all proportion. We then have to ask ourselves if those who cling so tenaciously to the fetish of this particular symbol are not confusing the symbol with what it symbolizes, that is, in this case, confusing the father image with God.

I have had a personal experience of this kind. At a worship service in St. Catharine's Church in Hamburg last December, we spoke of our Father and Mother in heaven. We received some letters afterward from Christians who —even though they realized that language is always symbolic—still felt it was going too far to introduce a change like that into the liturgy. In other words, when people are confronted existentially with the phrase "God the mother," when it is actually said, publicly and clearly, they are offended and say that's going too far. These points where people begin to take offense, then, are highly revealing, for they show us where the symbol and the symbolized have merged in people's consciousness. When one mode of language has become so dominant and assumed a compulsive character, all the other symbolic words that human beings have used to convey their experiences of God are shoved into the background, or they are placed on some lower level in the hierarchy.

Of course it is possible to speak of God as a mother, people say, as though it somehow disposes of the problem to say that hierarchically lower levels of religious consciousness make use of other verbal symbols; but, when all is said and done, the image of the father still remains the most important one. Pope Paul VI pointed out in a statement that received a lot of publicity that God was every bit as much mother as father. But, as I've said, in terms of religious practice we are still a long way from this relativizing of our symbolic language.

The question is: How can we escape from the prison this language constitutes? And it is a prison, this father language, this sexist language, this language that excludes women. Many attempts in this direction are being made all the time, and I can mention an example from that same service at St. Catharine's. At the end of the service, four of us, all women, spoke this benediction: "May God bless and keep you and make her face shine upon you and give you peace." All we did was substitute the pronoun "her" for "his" to suggest that it was a mistake to stay bogged down in the dominant sexist exclusivity and think of God only as a father. We do not mean to substitute a dominant feminist exclusivity, but in a paternalistic culture, language has to be turned on its head before anyone will begin to grasp what the problem is and to understand that human beings might choose another symbol to identify with.

These are examples of the tentative efforts women are making everywhere today whenever they become aware of their situation. The desire for a different concept of God, other symbols, and other hopes is crucial for those who need a different God because they have been insulted, humiliated, and disgusted by the culture we live in. It is not men who suffer primarily from the sexism of theological language; it is women, the other 51 percent of humanity. I feel that the relativizing of this absolutized God-the-father symbol represents a minimal demand we should make.

There are, of course, other symbols we can choose for God. If we want to continue the use of family-oriented symbols, we can call God mother or sister. But other symbols that have nothing to do with the family seem even more vivid to me, symbols that can be found in mystical literature. An antiauthoritarian theological language would be able to pick up the mystic tradition and carry it forward. The source of all things, the living wind—these, too, are words people have used to express their relationship with God without resorting to sexist or familial symbols. There are many more ways than we realize for saying what I have been attempting to say here, and for the sake of more communication and a better religious language, we have to change the authoritarian language the churches use when they squeeze a broad stream of consciousness down into a narrow channel. God is light, the water of life, air. Those are other symbols of the divine that do not emanate authority and power. It is absurd to speak of light giving commands. A God that is light simply does not command. A God of light is neither a familial symbol nor a symbol of power.

This kind of language speaks to other experiences in us. In the mystical tradition, there is no room for deferring to a higher power, for worshiping alien rule, and for denying our own strength. On the contrary, mystical texts often explicitly criticize the master-servant relationship; and their primary way of doing this is through a creative use of language.

Here, religion is a sense of unity with the whole, a sense of belonging, not of submitting. We do not honor God because of his power over us; we immerse ourselves in him, in his love, as mystical language often puts it. He is, as Meister Eckhart says, the fundament, love, the depths, the sea. Symbols from nature are preferred where our relationship with God is not one of obedience but of unity, where we are not subject to the commands of some remote being that demands sacrifice and the relinquishing of the self, but rather where we are asked to become one with all life.

The most important virtue in this kind of religion is not obedience but solidarity, for solidarity asks that we change the image of God from that of a power-dispensing father to one of a liberating and unifying force, that we cease to be objects and become subjects involved in this process of change, that we learn cooperation rather than wait for things to come to us from on high. These are all elements of mystical piety.

To come to my fifth and last point, mysticism means learning to yield up the self. Eckhart says, "And so I ask God that he make me quit of God." That is one of those paradoxical formulations which suggest that the traditional God that Eckhart had grown up with had become an imprisoning symbol. Any word that freezes our concepts, appeals to our willingness to be submissive, and consequently destroys our capacity to be at one with others and the All can become a prison.

Eckhart wants to become free of the false God, the Lord God, the commanding God, the God of power, so that he can become one with the movement of God in the world. He wants to become one with God in his pain, become vulnerable in his struggle, just as God is, live unprotected because that is how God lives. He does not want to be defending himself constantly and making defense and security our real gods that we honor in symbols of protection.

Take Luther's line "A mighty fortress is our God." There is something valid in that image, but it is an image that has been used in our tradition to keep us at a remove from life. If God is a mighty fortress, the rest of the world around it can go to rack and ruin while we sit inside the fortress, secure in a special place that remains untouched by what is going on outside.

Mystical experience is difficult to describe. One method the mystics used was to divide the totality of the mystic experience, the moment, the now, into different steps. The process is one of clarification in which the different steps toward union with the All are described. We can perhaps describe it as a yielding up of the self. If we say, for instance, "I give myself into God's hands," there are other implications contained in that sentence: I yield myself up; I leave myself in God's care; I depart from self, leave myself behind.

Learning how to do this was one of German mysticism's major goals, and mystics distinguished three steps in the process: leaving the world, leaving the self, leaving God. I will not interpret this now in the context of mystical religiosity, for I have dealt with this theme in my book *Death by Bread Alone*, to which you can refer later if you like.

For now I want to interpret this in the context of our culture, specifically, in the context of the counterculture or youth culture, where there are, I think, very clear mystical tendencies. Many young people are in fact leaving the world and have advanced quite far in their departure from the world. They have turned away from careerism, from educational requirements, from the Protestant work ethic, from the idea that you are a real and complete human being only if you have completed some kind of professional training, have entered the work force, earn so and so much money, and have this or that standard of living.

A number of young people are calling these norms into grave doubt. They have shoved aside and left behind the world of their fathers and mothers. They don't find that world with its careerism and fetish for education so important that one should sacrifice personal development, one's own life, one's ties with nature and with other people to it. These are some of the sharpest criticisms that are being leveled at mainstream culture by those who are leaving it, and I see these criticisms in terms of the mystical tradition. In their way, these young people are "leaving the world," and there are clear anarchistic tendencies present in what they are doing. Anarchy is another term that belongs in the context of this discussion, because mysticism has in fact often led to anarchism, to the forming of nonhierarchical societies, even if these societies have remained very small.

The second step, that of leaving the self, is one that these young people do not often take. If I understand this step correctly, it means that we have to strip ourselves of the images we have lived by and leave our egos behind. On its deepest level, it means that we have to put our own sadness, our own depression, behind us. Sadness and depression are what we often experience when we leave the world, and if we remain in this depressed state, we have not by any means left the self behind. On the contrary, it is this despairing self, this self no longer capable of anything, this destroyed creature, that comes to dominate us with a vengeance.

What we should try to learn from the mystics, then, is to leave the self, to put away depression, to make the self empty, open, and ready; for only if we are empty, the mystics tell us, can God fill us.

The last step in this process is to leave God. I take this to mean, in religious terms, that we have to leave the Lord in order to find God in our brothers and sisters. We have to give up obedience to find solidarity. We have to give up relationships of domination, even if our role in them is the servant's role. We have to overcome the master-servant relationship and become one with our brothers and sisters, and in the course of this becoming one, as Eckhart says, we become quit of the God who commands and dominates.

That would be a major step in the direction we have to travel. I think what we need in order to take that step is a new language, and feminists (both male and female) are working hard today to develop a language that says more clearly what it amounts to and means to leave God for God's sake.

And so, Eckhart says, I ask God to make me quit of God for God's sake. And with that I would like to close.

9
PATERNALISTIC RELIGION AS EXPERIENCED BY WOMAN

One of the names with which the Jewish-Christian religion refers to God is "Father." This symbolic attribute obviously has practical implications for people today. What are these implications? I am not concerned here with the way this symbolic representation originated in history, nor with its original meaning. I want to look at how it operated in history, and what happened once it was established.

The editors [of the volume in which this essay was originally published], two gentlemen who thank eleven other gentlemen for their "valuable suggestions and indications," came out with some composite terminology which can only be translated into English by "Father God" or "God as Father" *(Vatergott)* and a "Culture of Obedience" *(Gehorsamskultur).* Both these expressions annoy me intensely, and my objections can be formulated in three questions:

1. Did this obedience only create and determine a "culture"—or did it simply lead to a barbaric situation?
2. Can the word "father" still mean "God" when we have learned that God and liberation are mutually inclusive concepts?
3. Which exactly are the elements in the fatherhood symbolism we cannot do without?

The answers to these questions cannot ignore history and subjective experience.

Personally, I can see them only as a German, as a woman, and as somebody who tries to be a Christian at the end of the twentieth century. As such I refuse to deny my national, sexual, and socioeconomic identity.

This reaction springs from the fact that theological jargon does indeed distinguish the God of philosophy from the God of Abraham, Isaac, and Jacob but then has nothing to say about the God of Sarah, Rebecca, and Rachel. The "fathers of the faith" are reflected in the idea of the "Father in heaven," but the "mothers of the faith" are left in a limbo of obscurity: they are somehow "prehistoric," unremembered, forgotten; in fact, repressed. This repression not only affects the 51 percent of humankind who, as a result, never found their theological voice. It also has had a catastrophic effect on the theologians who are part of the other 49 percent, particularly in the way they express themselves.

The ignoring of the female component of the soul, the running down of everything that has a feminine flavor about it, has done more damage to the way theologians speak and write than any assault from the secular world. The purging and impoverishing process has led to the repression of the emphatic "wholeness," "awareness," and "integration" that marked the language of the gospel.

What is called scientific theology is usually conveyed in a language devoid of a sense of awareness. It is unaware of the emotions, insensitive to what people experience. It has no interest and no appeal; it has a flatness because it leaves no room for doubt, that shadow of the faith. One has only to read the male theologians' commentaries on Eve's conversation with the serpent in paradise, which make it appear as if any intellectual and sexual curiosity is something of the devil. Who would bother to have a conversation with that kind of serpent?

Any theology that wants to communicate with real people must, however, use a language that shows awareness, brings them and their problems into the dialogue, and is forceful. This grows from practical experience and leads to a change in being and behavior.

At present the language of scientific theology only very rarely achieves this quality of being truly alive. When it manages this at all, it does so in a roundabout way, in opposition to the academic establishment, which pursues the male-inspired ideals of neutralism, of being above party lines and emotions, and whose whole energy is aimed at making the problem go away. The student is trained in how not to say "I" when speaking scientifically. It reveals already a certain subversive talent when theologians (unfortunately, mainly white men) rediscover a way of dealing with their subject that shows awareness, is emotionally rich, and understands the individual.

I

The deepest difficulty I have with a culture based on obedience is linked with my national identity.

The history of the people I belong to has been slanted by a key event that occurred in this century. This event twisted language, words, ideas, and images precisely because it was central, a "key" event. Because of this, words and ideas have acquired an irrevocably different meaning. Because of this, these words and ideas have lost their original innocence. As one concerned with communication who has faced life after that event, I neither can nor want to forget this fact. This means I cannot overlook the fact that a given poem uses words that embody their own historical development. Thus star, smoke, and hair still meant something different in German even as late as 1942 from what they came to mean after the greatest crime and calamity in the history of my people.

My first serious doubt about a "Christian culture of obedience" is whether obedience is not precisely one of those ideas which are no longer valid after the holocaust. (See my critique of this ideology in *Beyond Mere Obedience*.) The question how deeply the conditioning of the Christian mind to an attitude of total obedience prepared the ground for Nazism is a matter for historians. For theologians the fact that Eichmann, who was enrolled in the German YMCA by his parents, constantly stressed obedience, as did Rudolf Hösz, whose father destined him for the priesthood, should be enough to rob this concept of all its theological innocence. Nor does it help to make a distinction between the "true" or "proper" obedience to *God* and obedience to *man.* Can one want and develop an attitude toward God that one criticizes in people in their attitude toward other people and human institutions?

Should obedience necessarily lead to a barbaric situation? This question is much wider than its mere connection with historical Nazism. Today "obedience" is seen in terms not of charismatic leaders but of the "market forces" of the economy, the use of energy, and growing militarization. It is true that the technocrats have long ago taken over the inheritance of the priests. But even in the new situation where obedience is preferably spoken of in terms of the "rules of the game," the structural elements of authoritarian religion persist and the remaining traces of religious education prepare the increasingly a-religious masses for an obedience from which all personal features based on trust and sacrifice have vanished.

This new computerized obedience has three structural elements in common with the old religious obedience:

a. acceptance of a superior power that controls our destiny and excludes responsibility for our own fate;

b. subjection to the rule of this power, which needs no moral legitimation, say, in love or justice;

c. a deep-rooted pessimism where man is concerned: the human being, incapable of death and love, is a powerless and meaningless creature whose obedience feeds precisely on the denial of its own innate potential.

The main virtue of an authoritarian religion is obedience and self-abrogation as the center of gravity, in contrast with a humanitarian religion, where the chief virtue is self-realization and resistance to growth is the cardinal sin.

From the point of view of social history, such an authoritarian concept of religion affirms society and has a stabilizing influence on its prevailing tendencies. In such a context authoritarian religion discourages any willingness to aim at greater emancipation and a critical attempt to rise above the established realities, also—and particularly—when these trends base their arguments on religious grounds: God's love and righteousness are less important than his power.

Authoritarian religion leads to that infantile clinging to consolation which we can observe in the sentimentality of religious art and the history of devotionalism. But this goes together with a compulsive need for order, a fear of confusion and chaos, a desire for clarity and control. And when religion is dying out it is precisely this rigidity which survives; it is the authoritarian bonds which mostly persist in a life that is understood as dominated by technocracy. The Milgram experiment showed that a vast majority of the ordinary people included in the research were quite prepared, under scientific direction, to torture innocent fellow humans with electric current, which is precisely what happens in a "culture" of obedience. Obedience operates in the barbaric ethos of fascism, Nazism, or technocracy.

II

The late Erich Fromm distinguished between humanitarian forms of religion and authoritarian ones. The historical Jesus, early Buddhism, and the mystics of most religions display the kind of religion that is not repressive, not based on one-sided and asymmetric dependence, but operates with a force which springs from the inner life. It is precisely here that one begins to question the social-psychological implications of the father symbol.

Why do people worship a God whose supreme quality is power, whose interest lies in subjection and who fears equality?

Theologians, accepting such a being, to be addressed as "Lord" and not content with just power, are bound to ascribe omnipotence to it.

The main objections of a developing feminist theology to the existing kind of theology are directed against phallocratic fantasies and the worship of power. Why should we worship and love a being which not only fails to rise above the moral level of a past male-dominated culture but even turns it into an establishment?

May I put this in terms of my own theological development? My objections to the divine "superpower" began to make themselves felt when I visited Auschwitz. I published my first book, called *Christ the Representative: An Essay in Theology After the Death of God*, in 1965. There I followed Bonhoeffer and was radical and Christocentric.

God himself, whether acting or speaking, cannot be experienced by humans. So we should cling to the nondominant, powerless Christ who has nothing with which to persuade and to save us but his love. His very powerlessness constitutes an inner-personal authority; not because he begot, created, or made us are we his, but simply because his only power is love, and this love, without any weapons, is stronger than death itself.

My difficulties about God as father, begetter, ruler, and the manager of history grew as I began to understand more clearly what it means to be born a woman, and therefore "incomplete," and so to have to live in a patriarchal society. How could I want power to be the dominant characteristic of my life? And how could I worship a God who was only a male?

Male power, for me (as I have mentioned elsewhere), has something to do with roaring, shooting, and giving orders. I do not think that this patriarchal culture has done me any more damage than other women. It only became constantly more obvious to me that any identification with the aggressor, the ruler, the violator, is the worst thing that can happen to a woman.

Moreover, the father symbol cannot have the same fascination for those who will never be a "father." Even power replaced by the mercy of the kind and gentle father, or of the kind slaveowner who is loved and respected by his slaves, does not solve the problem.

Yet feminine piety is and will be a kind of "Uncle Tom" piety. But when women are subjected to functions and an obedience that have been laid down by males with regard to a God who is assumed to have fixed all this in "nature," then women's potential is destroyed and they will never achieve the full status of human persons. No "father" can liberate us—women—from the history of my people and the sexism of today's culture. So: Can the father symbol still adequately represent what we mean by "God"?

When one understands that anything we say about God is bound to be symbolic, then any symbol that presumes to cover the absolute must be relativized. God does indeed transcend our speech but only if we do not lock him up in our human symbols.

I quite agree that "father" is one way in which we can talk about God, but when this way is forced upon us as the exclusive way, we confine God in the prison of this symbol.

Because of this sort of enforced language, all other symbolic expressions that people have used to convey their experience of God are repressed or at least considered as of lesser value. It is true that Paul VI attracted widespread attention when he once said that God was at least as much "mother" as "father." But in religious practice we are still far from having achieved this relativization of symbolic speech. When we began a service in St. Catharine's Church, Hamburg, with "In the name of the Father and the Mother, the Son, and the Holy Spirit" there was a fierce argument about whether this kind of language should be allowed. Changing the sacred language of the liturgy is one way of escaping from prison and so is seen as a threat. Four women together pronounced the blessing: "May God bless you and watch over you. May she let the light of her countenance shine upon you, and may she grant you peace."

This shows the way in which everywhere women, aware of their situation, are groping for a solution. The wish for another way of presenting God, for other symbols and expectations, is important for those who feel themselves offended, humiliated, and disgusted by the culture in which we live. It is not the male who is the first victim of the sexism that has molded the language of theology.

The relativization of such an absolutized symbol as "father" is the least we can ask for. Other symbols can be used for God. We can address God as "mother" or "sister," if we want to confine ourselves to family terminology. But it seems to me that symbols taken from nature are in any

case much clearer because they are innocent of any authoritarian implication.

Theological language could get rid of the streak of domination if it looked at the language of the mystics.

"Source of all that is good," "life-giving wind," "water
of life," "light" are all symbols of God that do not imply
power or authority and do not smack of chauvinism. There
is no room for "supreme power" domination or the denial
of one's own validity in the mystical tradition. It often
explicitly criticizes the lord-servant relationship, which has
been superseded, particularly by the mystics' inventive use
of language.

In this tradition religion means the experience of being
one with the whole, of belonging together, but never of
subjection. In this perspective people do not worship God
because of his power and domination. They rather want to
"drown" themselves in his love, which is the "ground" of
their existence. There is a preference for symbols like
"depth," "sea," and those referring to motherhood and to
nature at large. Here our relationship to God is not one of
obedience but of union; it is not a matter of a distant God
exacting sacrifice and self-denial, but rather a matter of
agreement and consent, of being at one with what is alive.
And this then becomes what religion is about. When this
happens, solidarity will replace obedience as the dominant
virtue.

III

Are there any elements in this father symbolism as applied to God which a liberating theology cannot do without?
Is a personalist terminology here preferable to other possible symbols? Do we need to explain the relationship between God and man through this father symbol?

In a patriarchal culture the father represents the dependence of the individual. It is rooted in the biological fact

that the young of the human species are begotten and need care and protection for a long time. But does our protracted childhood justify a religious language that is essentially based on the parent-child relationship? And is the underrating of the mother in this relationship, as if it is only the father who provides the original begetting and survival, not an additional emphasis on the authoritarian element in this relationship? In Judaism the father image is based on his function as head of the family, with definite legal, religious, pedagogical, and economic power.

The father is judge, priest, teacher and controls the means of production.

Whoever lives in this culture and addresses God as father has personally experienced these various ways of being dependent, and for a woman this experience is still much more acute. Only gentleness and compassion, the other feature of the father symbol, can make this dependency tolerable.

This linking of absolute authority with mercy is the main characteristic of God as father. Everywhere paternal kindness and judicial power constitute the two poles that determine the father image. But when the accumulation of power based on this combination of biology with sociology is collapsing and rapidly becoming a "thing of the past," does this not also deprive any religious exaggeration of these functions of rational foundation? Is there then something in the father image we cannot do without?

It seems to me that at the core of all feminist philosophy or theology there lies this matter of "dependency." Do we need a liberating concept, a central value, that women themselves should discover? Or are there ways of being dependent which simply cannot be ignored? Is it a good thing to make oneself emotionally independent, or would this only lead us to the position of the male with his superficial ties who would not dare attack the ideologized independence of the male heroes? What does it mean anthropologically to be dependent? What does it mean in social life? The area covered by this interfeminist debate is also the area where decisions have to be made in theology. Is this dependency only a repressive inheritance from the past or is it part of the simple fact that we are "created"?

We have not made or planned ourselves, nor have we chosen our own place in history or geography. Our whole life is inserted between a "before" and an "after"; we are essentially integrated in this process, and we can only tear ourselves out of the implied relationships at our own peril. Ontologically we are not and never are alone. There is a "one world" we have to believe in; there is a universal "wholeness" and a universal purpose.

Is it not possible that addressing God as father expresses precisely this interdependence? One of the texts by Simon Dach (1605–1659) set to music by Johann Sebastian Bach runs as follows:

> Though master, only through thy power,
> Brought to the light by thee.
> Through thee my life is still in flower,
> My years and months through thee to be.
> Thou knowest when I have to leave
> This vale of tears. And where.
> Or when my life will end.
> Thou, Father, knowest: Thou art there.
> (Freely translated)

Here the "power" of the Lord, called "Father" in the last line, accurately shows that it refers to the power to beget, create, sustain, and, in the end, terminate life. We have no control over either our birth or our death. So, to address God as father means that life and death are not left to the contingencies of our existence. To see the world as creation means to see it as willed, planned, and "good." If speaking of God as father helps us not simply to face our transiency as something to overcome, but to affirm our dependency and to accept our finite and creaturely condition, then there is no reason why we should not do so. Symbols taken from family life can be liberating if they interpret our dependence theologically as expressing our trust in father and mother.

Symbols for God, taken from family life and speaking of God our father and God our mother, can be liberating not because they cushion the inimical and oppressive features of patriarchism but because they integrate us with nature and the human family. Then calling God "father" is no longer a matter of sociological exploitation, of fixing people in predetermined social roles and endorsing a false dependency; it will no longer be used to turn childlikeness into infantilism. It will rather enable us to have confidence in that life which transcends our own lifetime. It will even lead us to trust Brother Death.

10
ADAM AND EVE:
A LITURGICAL FANTASIA

University Worship Service
St. Catharine's Church, Hamburg
Second Sunday of Advent
December 9, 1979

PRELUDE: Flute

GREETING: D. Soelle

In the name of the Father and the Mother, the Son, and the Holy Spirit. Amen.

I welcome you to this service, which has been written by women for women. We have tried to take the Bible literally in it:

"So God created man in his own image, in the image of God he created him; male and female he created them" (Gen. 1:27). If we are all created in God's image, then God is every bit as much woman as he is man. We have therefore taken the liberty of changing some of the phrasing of the liturgy so that it is valid for that 51 percent of humanity that is usually not taken into account in church services.

The new self-confidence that women feel has done more than just sharpen our sensitivity to language. It has also led us to new self-expression for our bodies and feelings. We want to attend worship services without keeping our bodies and feelings out of the church or checking them at the door. We would like to ask you to be cognizant of your body here, to feel its presence. A worship service is not a board meeting where men sit around a table and talk. To make this clear, let's stand up when we sing. That is the natural posture for singing. If we remain seated, we negate singing and show that we don't really want to join in it. We especially urge you to sing along with gusto, both in unison and alternately, to help overcome traditions that are inimical both to the body and to music. We would like to have the first two hymns sung alternately by men and women. We'll sing the first and last verses together. The women will sing the second verse, the men the third, and so on alternately.

Because of a technical malfunction we do not have enough copies of the program for this service and of the texts and prayers to be used in it. We would appreciate it if you could summon up enough human feeling to distribute these sheets so every two of you can share one. There are people here who do not have a copy, but we need all of you to act, sing, pray, and read together with us. We want everyone to participate. And for this reason I ask you to see that a program is accessible to everyone here.

Perhaps this will help us achieve the other goal that we as women have: to include not only our bodies but also our emotions, not to hide them. We do not want either to hide or to repress the emotions we feel. In other words: Show your anger if you feel angry; show your joy if you feel joyful. Express your feelings to your neighbor. Don't think that this is a holy place or that holiness consists in sitting quietly in your place in stillness, silence, and isolation. I think that emotions are living things only if we share them, that everything has to be shared to be alive. We can have them only by sharing them. And so I hope you will all try to express, verbally or nonverbally, what you are feeling.

HYMN: "O Savior, Rend the Heavens Wide"

TEXT: GENESIS 2:18–23:

> Then the LORD God said, "It is not good that the man should be alone; I will make him a helper fit for him." So out of the ground the LORD God formed every beast of the field and every bird of the air, and brought them to the man to see what he would call them; and whatever the man called every living creature, that was its name. The man gave names to all cattle, and to the birds of the air, and to every beast of the field; but for the man there was not found a helper fit for him. So the LORD God caused a deep sleep to fall upon the man, and while he slept took one of his ribs and closed up its place with flesh; and the rib which the LORD God had taken from the man he made into a woman and brought her to the man. Then the man said,
>
> "This at last is bone of my bones
>   and flesh of my flesh;
> she shall be called Woman,
>   because she was taken out of Man."

The reading is interrupted. The last verse draws objections from the congregation. Two women interject questions and remarks like: "What's going on here?" "Let me have a look at what you're reading up there."

"Why?" the reader asks them.

"Because you can't just go on reading stuff like that."

The two women come forward and climb up into the pulpit with the reader. "Let me have a look here," one says, then goes on to read:

> "And the rib which the LORD God had taken from the man he made into a woman and brought her to the man.

I don't get that. I can't understand that at all. And then it goes on:

> Then the man said, 'This at last is bone of my bones and flesh of my flesh; she shall be called Woman, because she was taken out of Man.'

"What do you think of that, you women out there. This book calls us wo-men!"

"Created for man!"

"And created second!"

"A helper for man!"

"And why? Because there wasn't anything better around. The animals weren't good enough for him."

"And made out of a rib? When I hear that, all I can think of is spare ribs, pork chops, slaughterhouses. Yuck!"

"So what's all this supposed to add up to, I'd like to know. Is it supposed to mean that we women are inferior and subordinate to men?"

"You know, now that I think of it, there's a passage like this in the New Testament, too. It's in I Corinthians:

> For a man ought not to cover his head, since he is the image and glory of God; but woman is the glory of man. (For man was not made from woman, but woman from man.) (I Cor. 11:7–8)

That's it. We've heard that story before.

> (Neither was man created for woman; but woman for man.) (v. 9)"

"Geez! Who wrote that?" (Laughter from the congregation)

"Paul."

"Typical!" (Laughter)

"But you can find even worse. Just see what he has to say to Timothy:

Let a woman learn in silence with all submissiveness.
I permit no woman to teach or to have authority over
men; she is to keep silence. For Adam was formed
first, then Eve, and Adam was not deceived, but the
woman was deceived and became a transgressor. (I
Tim. 2:11–14)"

"Listen, have we women ever really noticed what our
place is in our church?"

"In *our* church? Can this still be *our* church?"

"I don't want to have anything more to do with this
church."

"Let's go!" (Applause)

The three women go down the center aisle and leave the
church.

INTERLUDE, during which a flute piece by Honegger is
played:

Two women who have helped prepare the service come
forward to the pulpit, using the same center aisle the other
three have used to leave the church.

INTRODUCTION TO THE READING OF GENESIS 3:

We had actually planned this quiet, contemplative music
for later in the program. Perhaps you noticed that in your
programs. We wanted to let these three women's anger
hang in the air for a few minutes, for these texts that we
have heard here genuinely anger me as a woman. When I
hear that I'm supposed to keep silent and remain in subjection, I can't just let that go by.

You may say that these are old texts written a long time
ago and that what they say doesn't hold true anymore. But
I feel that this story about Eve and the serpent and the
apple has by no means lost its force today. We can see that
in prejudices and stereotypes. We women are supposedly
susceptible to seduction. We are sly and deceptive. We are
not trustworthy.

We have reread this old story, and we see it differently from the way we were taught to read it. Adam and Eve are in paradise. They don't have to do anything, and in fact there isn't anything to do because they have everything they need. There is only one limitation placed on them: God has reserved the tree of knowledge for himself. But it is, of course, this very tree that awakens Eve's curiosity. She wants to experiment; she wants to know what good and evil are. She takes the apple. And what happens?

Eve acted. She dared to do something. She took the chance of becoming guilty. But in doing so, she began living as a human being. She accepted the freedom to decide and to act. And after the so-called Fall, the Bible does not call her "woman" anymore but Eve, which means "mother of all who live."

Now we will read this story again together. Let's stand up to do this, and let's divide the roles up this way: We will all read together what God and the serpent say. The women will read what Eve says, and the men will read what Adam says.

Now the serpent was more subtle than any other wild creature that the LORD God had made. He said to the woman, "Did God say, 'You shall not eat of any tree of the garden'?" And the woman said to the serpent, "We may eat of the fruit of the trees of the garden; but God said, 'You shall not eat of the fruit of the tree which is in the midst of the garden, neither shall you touch it, lest you die.' " But the serpent said to the woman, "You will not die. For God knows that when you eat of it your eyes will be opened, and you will be like God, knowing good and evil." So when the woman saw that the tree was good for food, and that it was a delight to the eyes, and that the tree was to be desired to make one wise, she took of its fruit and ate; and she also gave some to her husband, and he ate. Then the eyes of both were opened, and they knew that they were naked; and they sewed fig leaves together and made themselves aprons.

And they heard the sound of the LORD God walking in the garden in the cool of the day, and the man and his wife hid themselves from the presence of the LORD God among the trees of the garden. But the LORD God called to the man, and said to him, "Where are you?" And he said, "I heard the sound of thee in the garden, and I was afraid, because I was naked; and I hid myself." He said, "Who told you that you were naked? Have you eaten of the tree of which I commanded you not to eat?" The man said, "The woman whom thou gavest to be with me, she gave me fruit of the tree, and I ate." Then the LORD God said to the woman, "What is this that you have done?" The woman said, "The serpent beguiled me, and I ate." (Gen. 3:1–13)

FLUTE: "Syrinx," by Debussy

SERMON ON GENESIS 3:13–24: D. Soelle

Sisters and brothers! It is not easy to be a woman, to be committed to the Judeo-Christian tradition, and to want to become a full human being. These three things—being a woman, being a Christian, and becoming a human being—are at odds with each other. Our identity is not given to us intact; we cannot take it for granted. In many languages the word "man" is the equivalent of "human being." In Hebrew, the name Adam can have both these meanings: Made of *adama*, or earth, Adam is a "human being," the "other" that God created in his own image. But Adam is also "man," for whom woman is the "other." In no language I know of is the word "woman" the equivalent of human being.

We women live in a tradition that insults us. We are ribs, witches, bra-burning women's libbers—the context our culture assigns to us insults us. We are a part, not a whole;

we are the "second sex," not the first. We are B and not A; or, as Karl Barth's classic definition of this relationship puts it, we are "after and below man." In the first report of the creation, it is Adam who speaks. The woman remains silent and is praised, a familiar story. This tradition of insult runs deep, and it has left its mark on the life of every single woman in this room. It has taught us to derive our identity from our husbands, just as we have had to take our husbands' names for much of our history. The minor change in our laws that makes this no longer the case has not done much to change our real situation.

Let me give a personal example. A woman friend said to me recently in a letter: "I sometimes don't bother to ask you how things are with you because I know you talk over your problems with your husband, as if it were he who defines how things are with you." This remark gave me a lot to think about. I had considered myself much more emancipated than I really am. And that is true of a lot of us. It is the inevitable result of that tradition of insult that grants women their identity, their truth, their relationship to God only by way of a man.

But are we women marked by the tradition of insult alone and nothing else? I personally see a struggle between two traditions in the creation story; and in the group of women who prepared this service, a turning point came when one woman pointed out in our second meeting that things were really not so bad after all and that Genesis 3 was quite different from the way we usually see it. It is the woman who is the key figure. She is no longer just a mute part of the man, an object; it is she who acts and debates with the serpent, much to the vexation of all male theologians. After all, you're not supposed to talk with a creature like that. And the woman learns something from this debate, namely, that knowledge will not kill her. And her insatiable curiosity drives her on to learn other things that will change her life. "The woman saw that the tree was good for food, and that it was a delight to the eyes, and that the tree was to be desired to make one wise." Food, aesthetic pleasure, and wisdom—sexual and intellectual curiosity are one here. The eyes of both the man and the woman are opened now, and they realize that they are naked.

In opposition to the tradition of insult, then, there is one of liberation. Schiller regarded the so-called Fall as the happiest moment in the history of the world. The words "sin" and "fall" do not appear in the Genesis story. We do read, though, that Adam and Eve were sent forth and driven out of the garden. Being driven out is what happens to us when we are born. The fetus is driven out of the womb where it was nourished and could live and breathe without any effort on its part. But when we are driven out, life begins; we encounter work, care, sexuality.

Adam and Eve leave the garden and emerge into the cold and harshness of life. Coming out is a phrase that has assumed great importance in gay liberation. It means that people no longer keep their sexuality a secret and no longer suffer the humiliating and self-destructive effects that such secrecy entails. Coming out is liberation. Let us read the story of Adam and Eve as a coming out. The first human beings come out and discover themselves; they discover the joy of learning, the pleasures of beauty and knowledge. Let us praise Eve, who brought this about. Without Eve we would still be sitting in the trees. Without her curiosity we would not know what knowledge was.

In the Jewish tradition, there is a morning prayer in which every man, every adult male, thanks God for having created him a man. Let's add a new prayer today. Let's say: I thank you for creating me a woman. I thank you that I was born and driven out from my mother's womb. I thank you for the tree of knowledge. I will eat of this tree until I die.

But isn't there something missing in this interpretation?

Didn't God curse Adam and Eve for their disobedience and their coming out?

I will continue reading from Genesis 3 now, starting at the point where we left off in our joint reading.

> Then the LORD God said to the woman, "What is this that you have done?" The woman said, "The serpent beguiled me, and I ate." The LORD God said to the serpent,
> > "Because you have done this,
> > > cursed are you above all cattle,
> > > and above all wild animals;
> > > upon your belly you shall go,
> > > > and dust you shall eat
> > > > all the days of your life.
> > > I will put enmity between you and the woman,
> > > > and between your seed and her seed;
> > > he shall bruise your head,
> > > > and you shall bruise his heel."
>
> To the woman he said,
> > "I will greatly multiply your pain in
> > > childbearing;
> > > in pain you shall bring forth children,
> > yet your desire shall be for your husband,
> > > and he shall rule over you."
>
> And to Adam he said,
> > "Because you have listened to the voice of
> > > your wife,
> > > and have eaten of the tree
> > of which I commanded you,
> > > 'You shall not eat of it,'
> > cursed is the ground because of you;
> > > in toil you shall eat of it all the days of your
> > > > life;
> > thorns and thistles it shall bring forth to you;
> > > and you shall eat the plants of the field.
> > In the sweat of your face
> > > you shall eat bread

> till you return to the ground,
>   for out of it you were taken;
> you are dust,
>   and to dust you shall return."
>   (Gen. 3:13–19)

This part of the story doesn't seem very compatible with the tradition of liberation. It explains why life is so full of care and pain. The key words in this part of the text are curse, enmity, pain, rule, sweat. The tradition of insult comes to the fore again here. Adam will be punished his life long because he followed Eve's initiative just this one time. Eve, who will share Adam's curse in having to work too, will be doubly punished because she will also bear her children in pain and have to submit to her husband. Work and sexuality, the most important areas of life for adult human beings, are described as curses and put under a negative sign. And within the tradition of oppression, these curses have been gradually codified into humankind's fate, as if thorns and thistles, labor pains, and the subjection of one part of humanity to another were necessary and inevitable. That is what our tradition has selected out of this story and made use of. But if we consider the text more carefully, we see that these curses are not meant to represent eternal verities but that they simply describe the realities of peasant life in Palestine. These curses do not define the way things have to be for all time. The harshness of life, the enmity between man and nature, the struggle against nature, the rule of men over women—these are all bitter experiences. Freedom has its price. Every child is punished for coming out. Every human being who grows and leaves a stage in his or her life behind has to pay for that. But we should not let this realism of the Bible thwart our efforts to come out. We should not let it destroy our belief that the creation is good and that its ultimate goals are the reconciliation of man with nature and freedom from tyranny.

The patriarchical God who has lost his exclusive possession of knowledge because human beings have eaten of the
tree of knowledge is in an unhappy position. In the repressive tradition, God is jealous of his privileges, just as parents are when they see their children beginning to move
beyond them.

These are the final verses of Genesis 3:

> Then the LORD God said, "Behold, the man has be-
> come like one of us, knowing good and evil; and now,
> lest he put forth his hand and take also of the tree of
> life, and eat, and live for ever"—therefore the LORD
> God sent him forth from the garden of Eden, to till the
> ground from which he was taken. He drove out the
> man; and at the east of the garden of Eden he placed
> the cherubim, and a flaming sword which turned
> every way, to guard the way to the tree of life. (Gen.
> 3:22–24)

Our situation is that we have eaten of the tree of knowledge but that the tree of life is unattainable for us. We can
understand, gain knowledge, take responsibility, but life is
not in our hands. Eternal life is denied us; and our deepest
wish, which is to return to paradise, amounts to eating of
that other tree and becoming one with life.

When Christ drives away the cherubim that guard paradise so that we can return to Eden, this does not mean that
we will be able to live in a kind of Adamic innocence. It
means that we can participate more fully in life and so eat
from the tree of life. As long as we are here, we have
knowledge but no eternal and perfect life.

Is reconciliation possible between these two traditions of
oppression and liberation? Is God an oppressor who guards
his privileges jealously, or does he want to see us strong,
growing, coming out? Do we bring guilt down upon ourselves if we take charge and choose freedom, knowledge,
the unknown? Or are we—as both men and women—capa-

ble of becoming human beings together?

The ultimate message that emerges from the Bible is that God is on our side, that he wants to see us come out. He does not just curse us as we leave the garden; he also accompanies us. He helps us on our long road to becoming human. The verse I like best in this story is verse 21: "And the LORD God made for Adam and for his wife garments of skins, and clothed them."

It was cold in the world, and it is still cold. There is a doctrine in the Jewish tradition that says human beings should imitate God. They should be holy as God is holy. They should do God's work, which is to say they should practice justice. Let us do what God does. The serpent did not lie. It is possible to clothe the naked of our cold earth today, too. Amen.

HYMN: "Let the Earth Now Praise the Lord" (men and women alternately)

ANNOUNCEMENTS

HYMN: "O Lord, How Shall I Meet You?"

PRAYER:

We will pray together (All), as women (W), and as men (M).

All: By casting me out of paradise
You prepare me for the wide world.
You have thrust me out of the nest.
You sent me out.
You demand decisions of me.
You give me the freedom
to choose between good and evil.
You have breathed an unquiet spirit into my life.
W: You have created me a woman.
M: You have created me a man.
W: Let me, as a woman, be created in your image.

M: Let me, as a man, be created in your image.

All: Let us not cease to live
the freedom that you gave us
as your children.
Let us try, as woman and man,
to strengthen each other in love,
in our love for life,
in our love for your earth,
in our love for your creatures.
Let us try, as women and as men,
to teach each other justice
and truth,
to point out and forgive the other's failings,
to share problems
and speak our thoughts.
Let us live more and more
in your image.

SILENT PRAYER

PRAYER: Our Father and Mother who are in heaven . . .

BENEDICTION:

May God bless you and watch over you. May she let the light of her countenance shine upon you, and may she grant you peace.

POSTLUDE: Flute

This service was prepared by Kirsten Kleine, Inge Meinhard, Kristin Pfau, Dorothee Soelle, Gesine Wallbaum, Petra Zimmermann.

Mattias Dittmann played the flute.

11
THAT WE SHOULD
LOVE ONE ANOTHER

December 8, 1968

For this is the message which you have heard from the beginning, that we should love one another, and not be like Cain who was of the evil one and murdered his brother. And why did he murder him? Because his own deeds were evil and his brother's righteous. Do not wonder, brethren, that the world hates you. We know that we have passed out of death into life, because we love the brethren. He who does not love abides in death. Any one who hates his brother is a murderer, and you know that no murderer has eternal life abiding in him. By this we know love, that he laid down his life for us; and we ought to lay down our lives for the brethren. But if any one has the world's goods and sees his brother in need, yet closes his heart against him, how does God's love abide in him?

Little children, let us not love in word or speech but in deed and in truth. (I John 3:11–18)

The message of the gospel is so simple that any child can understand it, even if he or she is unable to read or write. It is so simple that many of our most subtle thinkers find it difficult to comprehend. The message is infinitely banal. All it says is that we should love one another. This banality is the heart of the new theology, the heart of the new and old theology. John says he is not bringing us a new message but the one we have been hearing from time immemorial. This is true for our present situation, too. John is not telling us anything new in the sense that what he has to say has changed at all. We have been hearing this message for as long as we can remember, and we find its simplicity and banality almost intolerable. The case can be stated even more simply yet. You all know that line the Beatles used to sing: "All you need is love." That is the gospel, nothing more. That is the central idea in the Bible. That is why we are focusing on this idea here and trying to shape our lives in accordance with it.

The tradition we stand in has modified this key idea, enriched it, reflected on it, made dogma of it. The tradition has added Christology and ecclesiology to it, the virgin birth, the resurrection and the ascension, the Trinity, original sin, and eternity. But the banal truth, the one truth that counts, is: All you need is love. In the course of time and in the history of religious reflection, this idea has been eroded away more and more, eroded away by a language we do not understand. We have to submit all the terms I have just mentioned here to a complex process of translation if we are to understand them at all. I do not think we can restore this language, this house of language. I think we will have to let this house fall apart, that we will have to abandon it in the condition it is in and build a new one on this one simple foundation: All you need is love.

I used to feel very upset when the opponents of the new theology said that we who advocate it were diminishing the gospel. The implication was that the gospel was a broader and larger thing than we made it out to be. My feelings about this are different now because I realize that there is some truth to what they were saying. We are indeed in the midst of a reductive process today, a process of taking things back and away. We are "diminishing" the gospel and we have to diminish it. But when we reach the end of this reductive process, we will not enlarge the old essence of the gospel by adding old or new dogmas. We will enlarge it by adding the world. We will try, within the context of our own generation, to open up and reflect upon this essence and create a new structure out of it. If, then, the reproach that we are diminishing the gospel is correct, it is so not because we are stripping away a few dogmas that no longer interest us but because we have left out too much of the world and are not yet able to define ourselves in this world in terms of the essential gospel.

That is our task: to reflect anew on the banality of the gospel, relating it to all the structures of our society. The field within which we accept and reflect upon the banality of the gospel—the field of our world, our society, our politics, our work—is a horizontal field. The tradition has developed the essence of the gospel in a vertical field, passing it down from above to below. But what was possible for the tradition is not possible for us. We will unfold this essence in the context of the world in which we live, in the ties that bind human beings to each other.

The essence of the gospel is contained in the idea that we should love each other, contained in this amazingly simple and banal principle. We should perhaps rid ourselves of our fear of being banal. But there is still another fear that works against the gospel, namely, the fear that the gospel might ask too much of us or—to put it theologically—

might mislead us into issuing nothing but laws and commandments and demanding unceasing exertions from ourselves. "You ought to! You have to! It all depends on you!" This fear no doubt arises from an understanding of Christ which, indebted as it is to a long-established and primarily Lutheran tradition, continues to be oriented solely to the superego, that is, to certain authorities, such as those of society, of our educational system, of our parental homes. This interpretation of the gospel has left a profound mark on us and brought us into conflict with what we ourselves really want and what we are capable of doing. I do not believe that Jesus addressed himself to the superego. I do not believe that the simple statement that we should love each other speaks to our superego. I therefore believe that the excessive demands and exertions some people fear are based on a misunderstanding and that this misunderstanding has arisen because we persist in thinking solely in terms of commands. That we should love each other is not a command but a message of good tidings. And it is absurd to ask people to love on command anyhow. Love does not require justification by any authorities that stand above it or outside it. Love justifies itself by and of itself.

If we consider now just what it is that I John is telling us about love, I think we can list the following points:

1. Love is a message of good tidings, a positing of our potential, a true liberation.
2. Love means leaving death behind and coming into life, for our life is dead if it is without love.
3. Love means suffering and death. Love cannot preserve itself but rather gives itself, gives its all.
4. Love is sharing and giving.

"But if any one has the world's goods and sees his brother in need, yet closes his heart against him, how does God's love abide in him?" (I John 3:17). I hope there is not a single one of us who can hear this sentence without thinking how many millions of people in this world are without food now and will starve to death. While we become richer and richer, while we, by virtue of our membership in the capitalistic Western world, get more and earn more, the Third World is plunged into ever-greater misery. There are concrete plans for reversing this disaster. The World Council of Churches Assembly in Uppsala suggested that 5 percent of all the churches' income be given to the hungry. The synod of the German Protestant Church in Berlin weakened, and therefore corrupted, this suggestion by including some of the things that we ought to give among those we have always given and by simply not giving some others at all. More important than this suggestion, which is more or less restricted to the churches, is the political initiative by which all the rich nations of the world would give 1 percent of their gross national product by 1970 and 2 percent by 1980. To date, we have given only 0.3 percent. This political goal is a thoroughly realistic one if those of us in our country who consider themselves Chris tians work for a foreign policy that would permit us, without asking for security, to give the hungry what they need. This political goal, which we are still a long way from achieving, is, in my view, a focal point where eternal life can become a reality in this world and for us. Eternal life is at stake in the here and now and nowhere else.

God and love are inseparable. It is not possible—and this is probably the gravest error of all conservative theologies —to tear God and love apart and to say that God is primary and permanent while love is some secondary, derivative thing. The gospel never tells us to believe first, then love. It describes the achievement of Christian life in terms of unity: In loving, we believe. In loving, we depend on something other than ourselves.

As you know, the many critics of the new theology complain that we preach "nothing but a little human kindness, nothing but love." And they ask if that is in fact all there really is. And if it is, what comes after death? If God and love are as closely linked as I have claimed they are, these objections amount to no more than cynicism. Faced with the reality of six million murdered Jews or the reality of a starving child, one cannot speak seriously of "nothing but a little human kindness, nothing but love," implying that these things are too little.

But since we all, at one time or another, have to number ourselves among those for whom love is too little, we have to ask what it is beyond love that we expect. What are all those people expecting who are looking for something else, who are, perhaps, faithful churchgoers or still maintain some kind of tie with the church? I suspect they are afraid. They want greater security than love offers, the kind of security that can be conveyed by words like "father," "peace," "eternal rest." They want answers to their questions. Having no rest, they want rest. After war, they want to know where peace can be found. I think these needs are genuine and justified. But the gospel revises these needs for us. To all those who want a father, eternal peace, a final home, and answers to all their questions, the gospel says simply and inexorably: "All you need is love." You do not need anything else; nothing else is asked of you; nothing else counts. This is the one thing that really matters. Everything else is peripheral; we can do without it. A yearning for security and for an eternal companion is understandable. But in Christ, we are relieved of this yearning. Christ said that our eternal companion is to be found in our earthly companions and nowhere else. To live, we do not need what has repeatedly been called "God," a power that intervenes, rescues, judges, and confirms. The most telling argument against our traditional God is not that he no longer exists or that he has drawn back within himself but that we no longer need him. We do not need him because love is all we need, nothing more. We will have to develop this essential message of the gospel in terms of the tasks that face our generation and the next one after us. We will have to demonstrate concretely what love means. Questions about the nature, the degree, the spheres of influence of love will prove to be immaterial. We will be struck by the fact that love is indivisible, that it cannot be broken down into sexual love, charity, and love in the social and political realm. We know already that those who condemn the powers of sexual love make other people incapable of the love we call charity and mercy.

If there is something we will be able to say about God in the future, it will be this: God is our capacity to love. God is the power, the spark, that animates our love. When we have come far enough to understand that, we will no longer be afraid of banality. Nor will we succumb to that heresy which says Christ addresses our superegos and demands the impossible of us, for we know once again now that he has always moved our hearts. We should stop looking for God. He has been with us for a long time.

12
A SOCIETY OF THIEVES
AND PASSERS-BY

Fall 1973

At a conference of German and French workers I met Victor, who told about his life. He had lost two ribs in an accident, and the doctor had forbidden him to lift heavy loads. He worked in the metal industry, and his factory was the only one in his small city in southern France. The plant manager transferred him to a different job where he worked together with another man, and there were often heavy loads to lift. Victor explained to his co-worker that he had been injured and could not help with the lifting. The other man thought Victor was goldbricking. Victor finally took off his shirt and showed the man the hole in his back. Then the man understood.

But after a few days Victor was transferred to still another job. He was a Communist, and the management was afraid he would influence other workers less sophisticated

than he was. In this job his co-workers were two much
younger men. While Victor was doing his best to explain
his infirmity, one of the two nearly ran him down from
behind with a loader. He was able to jump aside just in
time. Again he had to take off his shirt to prove his point.
Within one month he went through the same routine six
times: He explained, asserted, assured, and, finally,
showed what was there to be seen. The plant management
could not fire Victor, so it tried to get rid of him by shuffling
him around. But Victor would not leave because there was
no other job he could get. He had no choice.

As he was telling his story, I was struck again by what
physical shame—a sense of physical weakness or inferior-
ity—can mean and how it can be used to grind people down.
In Victor's situation of physical shame and economic dependency, he could not afford the luxury of a political opinion, much less of political activity. He was completely at the
mercy of his circumstances. He was a victim—exploited,
threatened, hunted.

Victor's story, too, is the story of a man who fell among
thieves. Jesus' story of the good Samaritan tells us about
the behavior of four different groups of people: thieves and
victims, passers-by and helpers. These are the four roles in
the model Jesus develops. And when Victor told us his
story, his purpose may have been like Jesus' purpose: He
wanted to find out which side we were on.

In a report about piecework in a radio factory, I was able
to learn what the situation of older female pieceworkers in
such plants is.

> Mrs. Heinrich is thirty-three years old. She has been
> a pieceworker for twelve years. She has a five-year-
> old son. Her husband works in the same plant and is
> a shop steward in the union there. Mrs. Heinrich
> would have difficulties if, at her age, she wanted to go
> to work for a different firm. After ten years, a woman
> pieceworker is considered old. If Mrs. Heinrich should

apply for a job at a new plant, the management would prefer to hire three young workers, train them, and accept the possibility that two of them might leave during their training period and the third after a few years. That risk is preferable to the risk of hiring Mrs. Heinrich, who, as an experienced worker, would learn her job quickly but who also, after twelve years of piecework, will be suffering from one or more chronic illnesses that may mean sick leave and lost time for the new plant. Mrs. Heinrich is fully aware of this; besides, she could not earn any more in a new plant. In the course of her twelve years, she has worked her way up to an hourly wage of DM5 (1970). In a small shelf next to her machine, she has a whole little drug-store, a whole range of painkillers in different strengths to dull her various pains and permit her to keep up her pace.

Mrs. Heinrich has been a pieceworker for twelve years. During this period, she has worked on the assembly line and on different shifts. It was also during this period that she had her child. Her earnings were at their lowest during her pregnancy because she could not do piecework. After the child was born, she did work for the firm at home. As soon as she could find a day-care opening for her baby, she was back at the piecework. . . . Mrs. Heinrich never stands up during her eight hours on the job. At the morning coffee break and at her lunch break, she stops five minutes later than the other workers and starts working again earlier. At quitting time, when the other workers are cleaning up their machines and gathering their things together to leave, she dumps another box of parts out on her machine table and solders another fifty tube stems. Mrs. Heinrich's job is one with a short cycle. She solders 3,140 tube stems a day.

This report explains how people get into a situation where increasing economic dependency keeps them from changing employers anymore. When these female workers marry, have children, and grow older, a change is practically impossible. Minors are paid an hourly wage; workers have to be eighteen to start on piecework. They "shove the idea of piecework aside as if pretending that they will never have to do it. Because their pay is not bound to the amount of work performed, they can get up from their work often, walk around in the hall and factory, visit other younger workers, and take smoke breaks. When minors become old enough to do piecework, they often respond by quitting. And they often say before this happens: As soon as I'm eighteen, I'm going to quit. They are hoping that the new plant they go to will not demand as high a quota from them. When they change plants they go through another training period of two to three months; then they have to do piecework. The initial quota is so high that when young workers start on piecework they simply cannot meet it. The only workers who can fill these initial quotas are those whose economic dependency is so great that they are forced to accept this job and no other."

In Jesus' story there are thieves and victims, spectators and helpers. The people who will read what I have to say here about the story of the good Samaritan are not too likely ever to have to do piecework. They clearly do not belong among the victims. I cannot say whether they should count themselves among the thieves or not, but however that may be, Jesus did not tell this story for the sake of the thieves. The Gospels contain some other stories specifically for thieves, like the one about the two criminals on the cross. Jesus did not tell this story for the sake of the victims either. He devotes only two sentences to the victim; then he focuses on the people who pass by. Jesus intended this story for people of the "spectator" or "passer-by" type. Perhaps there is one of you who is asking himself or herself right now what the pieceworkers in Berlin have to do with that man who fell among thieves on the road from Jerusalem to Jericho. What, indeed, do they have to do with him? "Who is my neighbor?" the lawyer in the story asks. And what does it mean to love your neighbor? How is my neighbor "like me"? Do not the pieceworkers themselves want to do piecework? Do they not have a "different nature" than I? Have they not become different through their experience? And why should all this concern me anyhow?

The question "And who is my neighbor?" is perhaps the most dreadful question a human being can ask. Those who ask it must have made themselves blind, for if they had used their eyes for only a moment, they could not even conceive of this question. They must have made themselves so deaf that they cannot hear weeping or cries of pain. They have become cogs in a machine; if they can ask this question, they do not know themselves. They have become unbrotherly; they do not believe in equality. They have become passers-by. The society in which we live often seems to me to contain only two of the possibilities Jesus suggested in his model: either thief or passer-by. The society of thieves and passers-by can drive people to such despair that the example of the good Samaritan remains powerless to influence them. Living among thieves and passers-by, many people feel it is pointless to act as the Samaritan did. So they take the path of blind and helpless violence.

I want to tell you still a third story now. It is about the woman who wrote the report about the pieceworkers in the radio industry. After it appeared, this thirty-three-year-old journalist came under suspicion of having connections with the Baader-Meinhof group.* When she was arrested, she was unarmed and offered no resistance. She was in good health at the time. After about a year of pretrial detention, she was on the verge of physical and mental collapse. Her

---

*TRANSLATORS' NOTE: The Baader-Meinhof group consisted of basically idealistic young people who, in the late 1960s and early 1970s, turned to terrorism as the only solution to the ills of German society.

attorneys wrote: "She is totally emaciated; with a height of 5 feet 8 inches, she weighs only 106 pounds. At more and more frequent intervals, she has spells of weakness and dizziness, heart attacks, and constantly impaired vision. Since December 11, 1972, Marianne Herzog has not been able to get up from the bed in her cell. She has a constant fever (but is not even given a thermometer), more severe difficulties with her vision, and pain. Whenever she tries to get up, she loses her balance and suffers chills." Her lawyers' request that a private physician be allowed to visit her was turned down.

According to the law, anyone held in pretrial detention is innocent until convicted. The purpose of this kind of imprisonment is to prevent the suspect's escape and make it impossible for the person to obscure the facts of his or her case. But because German prisons often subject suspects to total isolation from the outside world, pretrial detention can amount to systematic destruction of the prisoner's psyche. Total isolation means being alone on a hallway with no other occupants, being cut off from the sound of other human beings coming and going, being cut off from any kind of social gathering. It means exercise in an empty courtyard, accompanied only by an armed guard. Though a normal prisoner's mail may be censored, one is at least permitted both oral and written contact with the outside world and may have visitors. If one is denied these rights and cannot receive mail, and if only relatives are allowed to visit, such total isolation can take on the character of a clever method of torture. Marianne Herzog, in a state of total debilitation, was released from pretrial detention in the spring of 1973, but she was arrested again after only a month.

In a society of thieves and passers-by, the victims are hidden away and their fate is not mentioned. No one has seen them; no one has heard them. And the relationship between stories that are told now and the stories that Jesus told is obscured. Indeed, the effect that the story of the good Samaritan has is often that of preventing any more stories of this kind from being told. The worship of the letter and the paper of the Bible is so extreme that it prevents us from making different and better use of the stories Jesus told. We repeat and interpret the old story instead of truly retelling it, that is, making secular use of it as Jesus would have us do.

Why is that? Do we have nothing to retell because, in our stories, there are only three types of figures: the victims, the thieves, and the many passers-by who only look and then pass on? The story of the good Samaritan is a beautiful and comforting story. The third passer-by did not pass by but proved to be a human being. If one third of our population acted as he did, the kind of piecework and the kind of pretrial detention I have described could not exist anymore. But I do not know any good endings for all the stories about our times. What kind of endings would Jesus give these stories? Who has been "a neighbor" to those attacked by thieves, to the humiliated, to those cheated of their lives? Who has stood by them? Who?

In the society of thieves and passers-by more and more people are becoming spectators, spectators to others' lives but also to their own. Their only connection with life is in watching it, watching others play, watching others suffer. Jesus had a very clear purpose in mind when he told his story: He wanted to decrease the number of spectators and add to the number of those who feel sympathy and act on it.

13
BLESSED ARE THOSE
WHO FEEL FEAR

December 1974

My text for today is Mark 4:35–41.

On that day, when evening had come, he said to them,
"Let us go across to the other side." And leaving the
crowd, they took him with them in the boat, just as he
was. And other boats were with him. And a great
storm of wind arose, and the waves beat into the boat,
so that the boat was already filling. But he was in the
stern, asleep on the cushion; and they woke him and
said to him, "Teacher, do you not care if we perish?"
And he awoke and rebuked the wind, and said to the
sea, "Peace! Be still!" And the wind ceased, and there
was a great calm. He said to them, "Why are you
afraid? Have you no faith?" And they were filled with
awe, and said to one another, "Who then is this, that
even wind and sea obey him?"

Brothers and sisters, this story belongs in the genre of so-called natural miracles, that is, of stories that were often told in the waning centuries of the ancient world about great men who, by God's grace, had the power to control nature and, as here, change the weather. I feel, though, that the countermanding of psychological laws, which is to say the laws that govern in the jungle of society, is perhaps of more interest to us than the countermanding of natural laws. The truth of the matter is that our ship is on the verge of capsizing. I hardly need remind you of the population explosion, of the effort to achieve zero growth as the only rational response to that explosion, of the threat of unemployment. We cannot know for a fact that the next generation will be able to keep warm or have work. And we certainly need not mention the hunger that the majority of the world's population is suffering now. We do not lack for information on that. Our ship is about to capsize. That means the ship that is the world but also, and primarily, the ship of the rich, industrialized nations to which we belong. We know that the shortages and the distribution problems we face in the future will lead to new forms of hate, struggle, fear, and, indeed, of fascism. Our sleep is uneasy, even though we cannot single out and recognize any specific dangers. Fewer and fewer people enjoy peaceful, healthy sleep. We are afraid, and our fear takes many forms.

We can divide human fears into those we have always had, the ones that are simply given because of our situation as finite beings with infinite demands, and those that have social causes. But by and large these two kinds of fears are closely related. They belong together and both threaten us.

I read recently about a woman who works at a machine in a factory. Her foreman has the habit of coming up on her from behind, and whenever he does this, her whole body shrinks in startled reaction. This has happened six or seven times a day, however many times the foreman has come by, for thirty years. The woman has developed a tic from this, and now others see her simply as "someone with a tic." There are many kinds of fear we live with, and I am not referring now to the big, widespread fears like the fear of death or of guilt or of meaninglessness. I am speaking of the fears that arise from specific causes and social situations, fears you are all aware of, fears that oppress more and more people.

The story I have just read to you is a simple one; it is simple in the sense that what Jesus says or does is always simple yet difficult for us to act on. We can call the essence of this story fear or faith, and it is a story that asks us to have faith. Why are you so fearful? Jesus asks. Why do you not have faith? Having faith does not mean we no longer feel fear. We do not simply stop being afraid. That would be a very naive view of faith and one that disregards the nature of the human soul, which cannot be so neatly manipulated. I think that most people in our society deal with fear as they have been taught to deal with it. They use a kind of evasive strategy. They avoid fear; they do not admit they feel it; they pretend to be strong, for the ideal that many people try to achieve is that of the strong individual who harbors no doubts and strides through life with a firm tread and an authoritative voice. If I can refer to an advertising image here, I would say that the Marlboro man is the ideal that many people strive to imitate. If this image of strength, of always being in charge, is our ideal, then any show of fear becomes a sign of weakness we cannot permit ourselves, a sign of weakness we have to overcome. That is what I mean when I speak of avoiding fear, for fear that we avoid, fear that we repress, is not fear that has gone away. If there is any fear that cannot be overcome, it is repressed fear. Anything we repress recoils back on us and takes its revenge.

In our story, Jesus is able to sleep not because he is naive or indifferent but because his life is rooted in a feeling that we can describe with the word "faith." This does not mean, however, that he was without fear. We know from the Gospels that he sweated blood and wept tears. The early church felt both these features to be offensive, and some of the scribes who copied the Bible left them out because they did not conform to the ideal image of Jesus that these people wanted. They wanted a strong Jesus, not one who wept or sweated out of fear.

Psychoanalytic theory has provided us with an explanation for fear. Psychotherapists tell us that all fear goes back to the fear of separation, and some of them trace this fear of separation back to that key experience that every human being has, namely, to birth itself, that transition from a state in which it is dark and warm and we get everything we need without having to exert ourselves, the state of life in the womb, to a state in which it is bright and cold, one in which we experience and suffer hunger and thirst. This transition is the basis of the fear we experience over and over again later in life. The architects of churches have understood this very well, and most churches offer us darkness, warmth, and safety in a bright, cold, and hostile world. Later fears are linked to our fear of being separated from what we need: the fear, for example, of being abandoned by someone we love. This is, perhaps, a typical fear for many women, the fear of losing a loved one in a traffic accident. These are fears that are always with us and that all relate to the fact that we do not want to be separated from others, do not want to be left alone, do not want to be isolated. It is a deep need for us—indeed, our deepest need—to be together, to live in the company of others.

The fear Jesus felt was a fear of separation too. Think of the psalm he prayed at his death: My God, my God, why hast thou forsaken me? The fear of being abandoned by God is the most profound fear of separation we can feel. But everything we experience of sin, too, is fear of being separated from each other by guilt. In sin, we separate ourselves from others by dominating or exploiting them, and we then live separated from them. I think we should rid ourselves of the habit of regarding sin as a private affair that takes place primarily between individuals. I think the sin we are living in is sin that separates us from all humankind. We are the ones the fingers point at in the Last Judgment. We are the ones with the white faces and the long noses, as the Asians say; we are the rich, the replete, the powerful who watch—and get rich from—the ruination of others. This separation from the rest of humanity, this separation that makes the white people the most hated and despised race in the world, is rooted in our sin, which is to say, in the world we have built up out of our aggression and our desire for profit.

For most people, and I am thinking here particularly of young people and the future they have to look forward to, our world is dominated by two images. Life consists, on the one hand, of a factory or a huge office, a place where something is produced. Then, on the other hand, there is the department store or supermarket, where you can buy everything you need. Beyond those two images, there is no concept of the world. That is all life is. It consists of these two things. You can work and produce; then you can buy and consume. Apart from these two worlds or realms there is nothing else. I think this explains the fear of meaninglessness so many young people have, the fear that drives them to suicide or drugs or alcohol, for there is in fact no other plan for the world and for life in it than this truly frightening one. And so we are afraid of guilt, of meaninglessness. And our deepest fear is surely our fear of death, which represents the most drastic of separations.

Belief in Christ is a radical attempt to overcome fear. Why are you so fearful? Why do you not have faith? This is what Jesus asks the disciples in the ship, and this is what he asks us, too. Why do we not have the strength to overcome fear, to overcome all our fears of separation by not hiding them but by transforming them into something else that tells us we are not isolated and alone? God tells us: You are not alone; you are never alone; even in death you are not alone; you are never cut off from the flow of love; once you have entered this flow, once you have been touched by it, you cannot ever be isolated again; there is no such thing as separation from God. God is with us and will always be with us. He will infuse us with this flow of love so that we can never forget his love. Why are you so afraid? Why do you not have faith? Faith, as I have just said, accepts fear. It does not repress fear. It admits the existence of fear, but it does not leave fear untouched. It transforms fear.

If we recall the oldest visions of the kingdom of God, we realize that with the coming of that kingdom everything that has been will not be simply eradicated to make room for the new. Everything that is and has been will be utilized; it will be transformed. Swords and spears will be beaten into sickles and plows. The tanks and armored personnel carriers that we waste millions on in my country will be converted into school buses. Instruments of war will be made into instruments of peace. Our fear is an instrument of war, too, a weapon that we turn against ourselves. With our fear we threaten ourselves, we destroy ourselves, we hold ourselves in check. We become preoccupied with our fear and imprisoned in its vicious circle. Fear is a prison we lock ourselves into, making ourselves both prisoners and guards. But, faith tell us, we can transform fear. We can make a sword into a plowshare. We can make the prison into a kind of assembly room or a church, not the institutionalized church but a church in the sense that Angela Davis has given to that word: A church is a place where we can speak freely, that is, a place where we can speak without fear. We can rechannel our fear. We can redirect the great energy that our fears drain from us. We can use it to different ends. We can free ourselves from compulsive preoccupation with our fears. We can make a productive force out of them, an instrument of peace and justice. Blessed are those who feel fear; they shall create peace.

If we are to learn how to do this, we cannot just go to church as individuals, cannot live our lives as individuals. A genuine transformation of fear has to be undertaken in groups, and I have in mind here the techniques of group dynamics that take these and related problems as their point of departure. These techniques are a kind of forging process by which fears can be transformed. But then we must know, of course, if we want to begin this process of transformation, to what uses we want to put the plow and the school bus and the assembly room, all these transformed instruments of death. To transform fear and learn faith means two things today: It means to become more religious, more radical, to take faith more seriously; and at the same time it means to become more critical, more radical, to take the plight of the oppressed and exploited peoples of the whole world more seriously. It means to join in the real struggles, to engage in them together, and—for the sake of a greater vision—to make use of our greatest fears.

"In the world you have tribulation; but be of good cheer, I have overcome the world" (John 16:33). I think we misunderstand Jesus if we regard him as a kind of superstar who speaks to us from on high (as I, quite inappropriately, am doing in speaking to you from this pulpit). Jesus does not speak from above, and he does not convey this message as one who is high up speaking to us who are way down below and very small. Jesus is not our master; he is our brother and our friend, and what he says here—that in the world we will have tribulation and fear—is meant to help us move forward so that someday we too can say: In this world, built on competition and aggression, we are afraid, but we are under way to a new and different world. We—not only Jesus, but all of us who have then become Jesus Christ. Amen.

14
SHARE YOUR BREAD
WITH THE HUNGRY
1977

Is not this the fast that I choose:
    to loose the bonds of wickedness,
    to undo the thongs of the yoke,
to let the oppressed go free,
    and to break every yoke?
Is it not to share your bread with the hungry,
    and bring the homeless poor into your house;
when you see the naked, to cover him,
    and not to hide yourself from your own flesh?
Then shall your light break forth like the dawn,
    and your healing shall spring up speedily;
your righteousness shall go before you,
    the glory of the LORD shall be your rear guard.
Then you shall call, and the LORD will answer;
    you shall cry, and he will say, Here I am.

If you take away from the midst of you the yoke,
    the pointing of the finger, and speaking
      wickedness,
if you pour yourself out for the hungry
    and satisfy the desire of the afflicted,
then shall your light rise in the darkness
    and your gloom be as the noonday.
And the LORD will guide you continually,
    and satisfy your desire with good things,
    and make your bones strong;
and you shall be like a watered garden,
    like a spring of water,
    whose waters fail not.
And your ancient ruins shall be rebuilt;
    you shall raise up the foundations of many
      generations;
you shall be called the repairer of the breach,
    the restorer of streets to dwell in.

                    (Isa. 58:6–12)

Bible texts are best read with a pair of glasses made out of today's newspaper. Submerging oneself in a foreign culture and listening to an ancient language is meaningful only for people who are deeply enough engaged in their own time and who are attuned to their own world, a world which is, perhaps, comparable to the one the prophet Isaiah inhabited. Isaiah sees what is happening among his people and in his society. He sees people unjustly imprisoned; he sees people abused and oppressed, sees them suffer from violence.

We need not limit our thinking solely to totalitarian states today to find comparable things happening. Even in democratic countries there are people who are unjustly imprisoned. I know, for example, a woman who lives in a low-income housing project. She has eight children. Her husband works only sporadically. Every week salesmen come to this settlement selling furniture, expensive watches, and color television sets. This woman I know is too weak to withstand their seductive sales pitches. She buys things she does not need and signs contracts for installment plan payments. At first, she makes her payments regularly; then she forgets them; then she sticks the bills behind the mirror. Repeated warnings to her go unanswered. Not long ago, she was sentenced to twelve weeks in jail. The judge regretted doing this because of the children, but he had to carry out the letter of the law. The primary purpose of our laws is to protect property. In the eyes of the law, the protection of property is far more important than the protection of children. Isaiah says: "Is not this the fast that I choose: to loose the bonds of wickedness, to undo the thongs of the yoke, to let the oppressed go free, and to break every yoke?" We have no problem understanding what he means.

Isaiah is speaking to his people as a whole and not to the individual. His intention is political when he says that you should "pour yourself out for the hungry." If we let our soul be touched by the hungry, our reason and our imagination, too, would be won over to their cause.

"Share your bread with the hungry." We know precisely what that means, for the recent United Nations Conference on Trade and Development has told us. It means, among other things, that the wealthy countries of the European Common Market should prohibit the raising of sugar and should lower tariffs on the import of sugar cane. "Bring the homeless poor into your house." We know precisely what that means. We do not build our cities for the sake of the people who live in them but for the capital that grows there. Our laws promote conditions that make more and more poor people homeless. You are not to hide yourself from your own flesh, Isaiah says. Do not think that politics is too dirty a business for you. Speak out for the mute, for the children of the poor, for example. Our cities are like deserts; they are dying of banks and the palaces of insurance companies. "And your ruins shall be rebuilt," Isaiah says. "You shall be called the repairer of the breach, the restorer of streets to dwell in."

Perhaps you will ask: Don't we hear this same message everywhere? This is what the humanists and socialists keep telling us, and perhaps they say it even better. Like us Christians, they too are working to transform our world, working better perhaps than we. What, then, is so special about Christianity?

The first thing I would mention in response to this question is the language spoken here. It is a language that touches our hearts because it is not simply a catalog of political demands. It is a language that woos us, tries to win us over. It suggests to us the possibility of living a different life. The text does not command, saying: You have to live this way or that way. It suggests an option instead: You could live this way. It leads us toward a richer, more powerful life. It shows us images of human beings who are like kings: Righteousness goes before them, and the glory of the Lord follows behind them. It shows us human beings who are like fountains and like light, normal, ordinary human beings like all of us here, who have become builders of happiness.

The text speaks of the richness of life. Do not be sparing of yourself, it says. The more of yourself you expend, the richer you become. The riches this text speaks of are the riches of being human, not the riches of owning things. The riches of possession find their security in ownership, status, and privilege. This kind of wealth is a wealth of material things only, a wealth of the dead and ossified. And it is wealth acquired through the impoverishment of others. It can be preserved only as long as oppression and discrimination are the rule in our society. The rich person Isaiah speaks of, the one who shares his or her bread with the hungry and talks with the depressed, is not rich in things but in human contact. Such a person has many friends. But this is not an internal wealth that permits us to ignore oppression and poverty in the external world. The rich person, according to Isaiah's definition, is fully aware of injustice, oppression, and the destruction of life in society but does not make peace with these things. Such a person's life has direction, a clearly discernible tendency. His or her goal is that everyone be given a name, be called repairer, restorer. Anyone who gains brothers and sisters is rich.

Isaiah is not addressing underlings who receive his commands. He is counting on the strong, the rich, who have been slandered and denigrated so often in the Christian tradition. But the prophet is counting on people like this, and he spurs us on to claim the beauty of a true and fulfilled life.

The gospel—and the text I have read here is pure gospel —is a beautiful thing. It promises us a life without disdain of others and without disdain of self, a life without cynicism, a life without fear, a rich life in which every hour counts. "Then shall your light break forth like the dawn." If you are wounded, your skin will heal quickly again. Even in the banality of everyday life, in the drought of our petrified circumstances, you will be able to "satisfy your desire." Nothing will be without meaning. "Your gloom [will] be as the noonday."

This text does not make any new demands of me. These are old and well-known demands, but I am offered the chance to live this kind of life. It is possible to live this way. This is how I want to live. This is how I want people to think of me. This is the kind of name I want to make for myself. When I hear this text I know again that we are strong, that we can accomplish things, that we are not dispensable. We do not have to sit around all year singing, with Luther, "Did we in our own strength confide, our striving would be losing." We have a new song: "Then shall your light rise in the darkness . . . and you shall be like a watered garden, like a spring of water, whose waters fail not." This is the way things should be; this is the way they will be. I will have a name. I will get an answer. I will not be a helpless, fearful creature anymore. The truth of the world, the meaning of life will be obvious to me. God says in this text: Look! Here I am. I am not far away. I will not come to more fortunate peoples later. I have not come to more fortunate ones before. The meaning of all life is here and now: Do not hide yourself from your own flesh; then shall your light break forth like the dawn.

Christianity does not say anything that has not been said elsewhere in the world. "If you take away from the midst of you the yoke . . . " But it does add an infinite promise: Nothing is without meaning. If you give yourself up to the movement of love, your strength will grow. The more you share, the richer you will become. Whenever you give yourself up to the movement of love, love will be with you. There is a heaven here among us. What does it look like? Listen:

"Rabbi Mendel wanted to know what heaven and hell looked like, and the prophet Elijah took him to show him. Elijah led him into a large room where a big fire was burning and where there was a large table with a huge pot of steaming soup on it. Around the table sat people with long spoons that were longer than their arms, and because the people could not eat with these spoons, they sat around the table and starved. Rabbi Mendel found this room and what he saw there so terrible that he quickly ran outside." This room represents hell, and the interesting thing about hell is not that there is nothing or too little to eat there. There is plenty of food. The room is large. There is a place for everyone. A cheerful fire is burning. The terrible thing is that the people seated around the table and the big pot of soup will have to starve to death because their spoons are too long.

Have we human beings been improperly constructed?

Have we somehow been given unsuitable and impractical tools to work with? Is it our fate to have to struggle with these unusable spoons?

This is how the story ends: "Then Elijah took Rabbi Mendel to heaven and into another room where a big fire was burning and where there was a large table with a big pot of steaming soup on it. And around this table sat people with the same spoons, but they did not have to starve because they were feeding each other."

Heaven and hell look exactly alike in this story: the same table, the same pot, the same spoons. It is not fate, then, that favors some people and rejects others. We have all been given a spoon that is too long, one we can do nothing with. It is up to us whether we will be in heaven or in hell, whether we will receive a name, become a garden, be a light. It is up to us. We can choose.

15
REMEMBER THE RAINBOW

January 1978

Remember the rainbow. Imagine it: a huge arc reaching from the earth up to the sky and back down to the earth again. When did you last see a rainbow?

We have dreamed about, meditated on, acted out, and shared with each other here today the beginnings of a new life. A beginning has its roots in what has preceded it. When a child is born into the world, that is a new beginning, but it is one linked with the children who have come before. This is why I would like to remind you of the beginning of a new life thousands of years ago, of a time when a new covenant was formed for the sake of life. I am thinking of the period after the flood. The earth is still covered with water and devastation. A massive catastrophe has nearly destroyed all life. Those who have survived make a sacrifice to God:

And when the LORD smelled the pleasing odor, the LORD said in his heart, "I will never again curse the ground because of man, . . . neither will I ever again destroy every living creature as I have done. While the earth remains, seedtime and harvest, cold and heat, summer and winter, day and night, shall not cease." (Gen. 8:21–22)

The earth will not be cursed because of humankind. It will hold to its rhythms and seasons. It will produce seeds and harvests. It will not be buried under asphalt, not be poisoned and stripped bare. Our bodies will be touched by frost and heat. We will not spend our lifetimes in the constant temperature of heated and air-conditioned offices. The earth will remain the earth in spite of all those who sell it and lease it, plunder it and destroy it. We all know how easy it is for the desire for profit that lies so deep in the human heart to be a curse upon the earth. It is impossible that the earth will be cursed because of man. In this story, God is on the earth's side, on the side of a mistreated earth that will not again be cursed because of man. The promise of life stands with us against the prospect of extinction.

We are in harmony with the oldest of human traditions, those that relate how curses and threats, the extinction and destruction of life are overcome. This overcoming is reflected in God himself here. At first, he wanted to "destroy" and "curse," but now there is the beginning of a new life in God himself. He is converted; he changes.

In the name of technological progress, of what is Bigger, Faster, and More, we too, perhaps, have been honoring a God that can do nothing but visit curses upon us. The God of the Old Testament was at least able to change and stop cursing the earth. Will the Western, progress-hungry God that has to subject and exploit everything that lives prove capable of change too? Remember the rainbow, the symbol of God's conversion.

God went on to say to Noah and Noah's sons:

"Behold, I will establish my covenant with you and your descendants after you, and with every living creature that is with you, the birds, the cattle, and every beast of the earth with you, as many as came out of the ark. I establish my covenant with you, that never again shall all flesh be cut off by the water of a flood, and never again shall there be a flood to destroy the earth." And God said, "This is the sign of the covenant which I make between me and you and every living creature that is with you, for all future generations: I set my bow in the cloud, and it shall be a sign of the covenant between me and the earth. When I bring clouds over the earth and the bow is seen in the clouds, I will remember my covenant which is between me and you and every living creature of all flesh; and the waters shall never again become a flood to destroy all flesh. When the bow is in the clouds, I will look upon it and remember the everlasting covenant between God and every living creature of all flesh that is upon the earth." (Gen. 9: 9–16)

As I read this passage, God's bow used to be a weapon, a bow he used to shoot his arrows or lightning bolts with. But now he puts his weapon aside and uses this instrument of war as a symbol of his covenant. The rainbow becomes a symbol of peace to us and to an earth never to be cursed again. I realize that this does not make the cloud over Hiroshima disappear or permit us to forget that cloud. But the rainbow does remind me of the possibility of peace, the peace promised to us, the peace we can make. If God himself needs the rainbow to remind him of his promise, how much more we need it. We need signs, symbols, reminders. It makes a difference whether the rainbow is present in our lives or whether we see nothing but symbols of command: red—stop; green—go. Remember the rainbow—peace between God and the earth.

We need the rainbow because it is made of water and

light and because it touches both heaven and earth. Water, fire, air, and earth are the old elements. The North American Indians identified the elements with the four winds and taught that a human being had to walk in all four directions and had to touch water, fire, air, and earth to receive their gifts. Wisdom, trust and warmth, breadth of vision and the ability to see what is close to us, those are all examples of such gifts. A person who walks in only one direction, who receives only one gift, and who develops in a one-sided way cannot become a whole person. Remember the rainbow, the gift of fire, the gift of water, the gift of air, and the gift of earth. Remember the seven colors that, taken together, make up light. Remember that time after the flood; remember today and the beginnings of new life.

16
WHO AM I?
Texts and Meditations on the Question of Identity

Who am I? Animals do not ask this question. Their existence is, as we say, rooted in instinct. But human beings, many of them, ask questions like: Who am I really? How can I live so that it is really *I* who live my life? How can I keep my life from being dictated and lived for me by compulsions and routine? How can I become one with myself? Who am I?

I have selected some texts here that give very different answers to these questions, and I would like to use them to stimulate reflection and meditation. Perhaps some of you will be able to identify with one or another of these texts and say, Yes, I've thought that too; that's the way it has been for me. That's how I would like to be. That's what I would like to become.

Closeness and identification with others can help us to

know ourselves better. I'd like to begin with a Yiddish folk song sung by a little girl; and if I could have one wish granted me, it would be that everyone could join in this song and know exactly what the little girl means when she sings:

> *Sheyn bin ich, sheyn,*
> *sheyn iz mayn Nomen.*
> (Beautiful am I, beautiful,
> beautiful is my name.)

What a joy for a human being to be able to say: "Beautiful is my name." This is the joy of children, the joy of childhood, the joy we feel again in love. I sometimes say something similar to my youngest daughter: *"Du bist mein Schönchen* (You are my beautiful one)." And sometimes I even say: *"Du bist mein Siebenschönchen* (You are my seven-times-over beautiful one)." But let's hear what else this Jewish child from an eastern European *shtetl* sings:

> A pretty girl am I,
> red socks I wear,
> money in our pockets,
> wine in our bottles,
> milk in our jugs,
> babies in our cradles,
> all of them cry: beautiful,
> beautiful am I, beautiful.

What does it mean for a child to grow up in a world where a song like this is sung? What does it mean to learn and sing such a song? Who I am is not determined by me alone but also by the interpretation the world around me puts on me. Were my parents eager to have me, or was I an unwanted child? Am I the prime object of their love and protection, or do I come far behind the car? And with this interpretation that is already given, I do not mean just the one that my parents and those closest to me give to me but also the one that society puts on me. The institutions and customs of a society convey a message, an interpretation of its life, to every child. They can tell the child: You are important. You are something extra special. Or they can say: You are superfluous. There is no room for you. Parking lots are more important than playgrounds for you. The sidewalk is not there for you to play hopscotch on. The arms industry is much more important than your school. For many children it has been determined long before they were even born that they do not need any place for themselves, that they have nothing to say, and that they should be as quiet and unobtrusive as possible.

In our song, things are quite different. The child has a place in the world of a comfortably functioning economy— money in our pockets, wine in our bottles. Life is worth living; happiness is possible; the self is beautiful. God said on the seventh day of creation that everything was very good. This song concurs with that. It expresses what a happy childhood gives a person for life: trust in the reliability of the world. Tomorrow will be as yesterday was. There will be wine in the bottles, milk in the jugs. Everything tells me I am beautiful, beautiful. That will not always be true for me, but that it was once true can never be taken away from me. At one time in my experience, life said a great "Yes" to me, affirmed my existence. This interpretation from outside forms and determines my own interpretation of myself.

An example of a favorable interpretation of my life from the outside world is the Christian baptism of children. What that ceremony really means is that the world says to the small child: You are beautiful. We want you with us. You were eagerly awaited. You are respected, endowed with dignity, worthy of being cared for and protected. Whatever may come, your name has been entered in the book of life. But there are many other interpretations that contradict those of glad tidings and also determine the shape of our lives.

The interpretation that we experience from the outside world as we are growing up can be quite different and quite destructive of identity. A young teacher in New York asked his black and Puerto Rican students to write down anything they wanted without worrying about penmanship, punctuation, or spelling; asked them to say just what they felt. Frank Cleveland, a seventeen-year-old student from Harlem using the pen-name "Clorox," wrote:

WHAT AM I?

I have no manhood—What am I?
You made my woman head of the house—What am I?
You have oriented me so that I hate and distrust
my brothers and sisters—What am I?
  You misprounce my name and say I have no
  self-respect—What am I?
  You give me a dilapidated education system and
  expect me to compete with you—What am I?
  You say I have no dignity, and then deprive me
  of my culture—What am I?
  You call me a boy, dirty lowdown slut—
  What am I?
  Now I'm a victim of the welfare system—
  What am I?
  You tell me to wait for change to come, but 400
  years
  have passed and change ain't come—What am I?
I am all of your sins
I am the skeleton in your closets
I am the unwanted sons and daughters in-laws, and
rejected babies
I may be your destruction, but above all I am, as
you so crudely put it, your nigger.

Clorox presents in a negative image all the things essential to identity: trust, self-respect, human dignity, the ability to form human relationships. He knows very well that these things are necessary in a truly human life, but there is no trace of them left in him. "What am I?" he asks over and over again, not "Who am I?" The outside world's interpretation of his life has overpowered him and destroyed him. He continues to defend himself, to strike out and scream, but how long can he keep that up? It almost seems as if the scorn and hatred he has experienced have forced him to scorn and hate himself. The strongest groups in the American black power movement have understood this and have therefore stressed the need for blacks to affirm their self-respect, their pride, their dignity. "Black is beautiful" was one of the key slogans in the civil rights movement, and it is reminiscent of the line "Beautiful is my name" in the Yiddish song. Who ever told Clorox he was beautiful? The mechanisms of violence, a brutal social structure, and self-destructive counterviolence all fit together neatly: Hatred follows on violence, and from this hatred that sees no possibilities of change and that is therefore not creative follows the self-destruction that is so familiar to us in the statistics that reflect the fates of young blacks in the ghettos. Criminality, depression, and drug dependence are the forms this self-destruction takes. Will Clorox be one of those young blacks who land in prison and come out again as hardened criminals? Is there no alternative? Does it have to be so that Jews will always think about money because the routine anti-Semitism of their environment projects this stereotype on them? Does it have to be so that blacks will be without dignity because a racist society has stripped them of their pride time and again? Does it have to be so that women who grow up molding themselves after one-sidedly feminine models will perpetuate the image of the sweet but stupid girl who cannot understand mathematics?

Who am I? And who decides that? Do I or do others? We probably come close to the truth if we say that identity takes shape in the interplay between external and internal interpretation. But to say this does not bring us much farther. If there is anything that I find encouraging and that gives me some hope for Clorox, it is the strength of his cry, the sense of injury he speaks from. "I am the skeleton in your closets." Someone who can say that can also break out of the closet.

After a long talk I had with a student about the intellectual climate at our universities, he wrote me this letter:

> The theology I encounter here does not help me achieve clarity about my faith. I do not come from a fundamentalist background, but the faith of my past experience has been naive and friendly. It enabled me to take part in political actions. But what do I run into here?
>
> Faith, prayer, and God are discussed in such tortured terms that nothing is left of them. I can understand the Taizé Community, and I can understand [Roger] Schutz. Those are clear positions. I can either identify with them, or I can reject them. I want to talk about God, not about the "ground of all being." I'm learning to differentiate so well here that I'm becoming indifferent. And if I say this, the theologians laugh at me. All they are willing to grant me is that I am in a "transitional phase," that my "childish notions will pass with time." What I run into here is either aggression or patience with someone who isn't as far along as everyone else. I thought that taking other people's questions seriously was part of scholarly inquiry. The atheists and the shilly-shalliers insist that I understand their questions, but they refuse to see my positions as questions for them. They label me as sick or retarded. They are always analyzing me: "That can be explained in terms of your social adaptation." They "understand" me so well. They can tell me

exactly where I am now and where I will wind up. I've lost my peace of mind not because too much is asked of me but too little in the way of piety, Christianity, and theology. I would like to live in Taizé or on Athos. In those places, there is a clear and unspoiled air of spirituality, an uncompromising purity. Prayer and meditation, life and concentration are not replaced by thinking and artificial, acrobatic interpretation. I am hardly an enemy of thought, and I am learning most in my seminar on basic philosophical concepts. But I object to replacing piety with interpretation. I am against those people who want to tidy everything up and interpret everything away. I feel robbed, I feel crippled by these interpretations that only water down my faith for me. And, curiously enough, I feel myself crippled politically, too. I used to belong to the left wing of the Young Socialists. I was a member of Amnesty International. We sponsored a lot of actions to benefit the Third World. Granted, I never felt altogether at home in the SPD [Social-Democratic Party of Germany]. But I think the religious uncertainty I am feeling is making me politically uncertain, too. I think the shilly-shalliers are training me so well in equivocation that it is becoming my basic attitude in life. Now I too am beginning to "differentiate" in my political thinking, not in the sense that I am moving toward the Right but rather in the sense that my enthusiasm and interest are fading. I am becoming more and more crippled. What can you do? In H. we opened a Third World shop. Retail stores financed it. The mayor patted us on the back at one of our promotional drives. The press reported "favorably" about this effort of some "idealistic young people." But what did it really amount to after all? I want to go the whole hog! Where can I do that? In the SPD? In some other group? I don't feel that anyone can accomplish anything here. People are always saying we make progress in "little steps," or they talk about "the long march through the institutions." But how long is that march going to take? And what have these people really done since they set out on it? We ought to be in Nicaragua. The first thing I read in the paper every morning is the report on Nicaragua. There's something there worth fighting for. It's clear what has to be done there. You don't have to sell your purity there.

This is the statement of a theology student in crisis, and I think what he has to say here is representative of what many students feel today. Their situation is complex, confusing, and ambiguous. They see people who can differentiate so well that they become indifferent, who interpret so well that they interpret everything away. "I want to go the whole hog," says this young man who, like so many in his field, cannot find any firm points of reference, any help. He is looking for something that he expresses in a number of ways: faith, clear positions, purity, the air of spirituality. What he finds is shilly-shalliers who teach him equivocation, and against them he rebels.

This letter bears witness to his rebellion. It takes courage to say things like this in public. It takes courage, too, to seek out authentic life in a derivative world. I can see this student before me. He reads only secondary literature, never primary sources. His professors stuff him full of ancient languages and knowledge about the sources of the Gospels, the social origins of the Reformation. But he has no primary experiences in the spiritual realm. He is starving for pumpernickel, but he gets Wonder Bread with the crust cut off and a vitamin pill on the side. He hears, for example, a psychoanalytical explanation of Kierkegaard's life, but he is not given what he needs to actually share Kierkegaard's experience for even a short time.

I mention this example because I am reminded of my student years. In my second semester I read, quite by chance as I recall, Kierkegaard's *Sickness Unto Death*. I was staggered by it. It called my life up to that point, my interests and goals, into serious question. It threatened me and took control over me. I lost myself in Kierkegaard and forgot everything else. Looking back, I would guess that I was in love with Søren, but isn't that the only way we learn something genuine, vital, and existential? In any case, I had daydreams in which I was Regina and behaved differently than she had.

But to return to the student who wrote to me: If there is anything I can wish him, it is an existential spiritual experience. His life is spent in talking about, knowing about. He can recite any number of theories, but they do not have any bearing on what his life is all about.

He expected more from his studies. Perhaps he wanted teachers and was given technocrats in instruction. Perhaps he was hoping for community—and, especially at his age, community can grow only around shared goals—and he found only small groups that changed constantly and moved in self-contained circles. He was looking for spirituality and purity in a world of neutralistic indifference. He was looking for spirit and found spiritlessness rampant. How important spirituality is to learning becomes clear if we consider how dry and conformist learning is if it is not spirited, high-spirited, enthusiastic; and, unfortunately, dispirited learning seems to be the rule at our universities today. The hunger of the young man who wrote this letter is spiritual. Who am I, he asks, in this factory disguised as a university? How can I find myself here where no self-discovery is asked of me? How can I learn faith where equivocation is the most important methodology?

Faith involves a kind of nonequivocation, a kind of directness and simplicity that, in complex situations, can seem rather naive. We are not living on Athos, that mountain where men submerge themselves in God, nor are we in Nicaragua, a country fighting a just revolution. But both these places represent something of that spirituality people need to find themselves. In both these places there is something of that purity this young man is seeking. But is he the only one seeking it? "Purity of heart," Kierkegaard says, "is wanting one thing, namely, the good." This young man's spiritual hunger is his desperate search for purity.

There is a poem by Dietrich Bonhoeffer that I have discussed once before, in my book *Death by Bread Alone*. The text reads:

> Who am I? They often tell me
> I would step from my cell's confinement
> calmly, cheerfully, firmly,
> like a squire from his country-house.
>
> Who am I? They often tell me
> I would talk to my warders
> freely and friendly and clearly,
> as though it were mine to command.
>
> Who am I? They also tell me
> I would bear the days of misfortune
> equably, smilingly, proudly,
> like one accustomed to win.
>
> Am I then really all that which other men tell of?
> Or am I only what I know of myself,
> restless and longing and sick, like a bird in a cage,
> struggling for breath, as though hands were compressing my throat,
> yearning for colours, for flowers, for the voices of birds,
> thirsting for words of kindness, for neighbourliness,
> trembling with anger at despotisms and petty humiliation,
> tossing in expectation of great events,
> powerlessly trembling for friends at an infinite distance,
> weary and empty at praying, at thinking, at making,
> faint, and ready to say farewell to it all?

Who am I? This or the other?
Am I one person today, and tomorrow another?
Am I both at once? A hypocrite before others,
and before myself a contemptibly woebegone weak-
    ling?
Or is something within me still like a beaten army,
fleeing in disorder from victory already achieved?

Who am I? They mock me, these lonely questions of
    mine.
Whoever I am, thou knowest, O God, I am thine.

Dietrich Bonhoeffer was thirty-eight years old, and he
had been in a Gestapo prison for several months when he
wrote this poem in July 1944. From all we know of him, he
must have been a man of great clarity, decisiveness, and
awareness, a very manly character in the best sense of the
word.

The images in the first part of the poem are unequivocal:
He is the squire, the commander who makes decisions, the
victor. He is all those things in a situation of the most
extreme degradation and humiliation. Rigor, concentration, conscious control are the hallmarks of the language
in the first part of the poem, where Bonhoeffer describes
how others see him. The sentences are parallel in structure,
and in each stanza the third line is taken up with three
modifiers, linguistic clues to the picture that others have of
the author. The interpretation from the outside world indi-
cates strength, self-control, superiority. But social identity
is only part of the answer to the question "Who am I?"
There is a tension between the external and internal interpretation of the self, between social and individual identity.
"Am I then really all that which other men tell of? Or am
I only what I know of myself?" What Bonhoeffer knows of
himself is that he trembles with rage, is powerless, empty,
and exhausted. This too is expressed in a realistic, re-
strained language that is classical in character, free of

sensual or expressive elements. Bonhoeffer's traffic with himself is devoid of sentimentality or self-pity. He steps back from himself, takes a cool, hard view, and passes judgment on himself. The defeated army that retreats in disarray before a "victory already achieved" seems to fore-shadow his death.

Here we see a human being confronting himself with two fully contradictory self-images, yet the strength of self in this identity remains unimpaired. To be in control of one-self, to be capable of organizing one's experience, to con-vey that experience in language, to orient oneself around a central point, to be centered—all these achievements of the self are present here, and yet a sense of wholeness is still lacking. The relationship between others' image and Bonhoeffer's own image of himself is one of equilibrium. The doubts and fears he feels are not given any more importance than the interpretation of others. Young people often think that no one understands them, that they are really quite different from what they appear to be. The adult Bonhoeffer says just the reverse: I appear to be more than I am. I seem to be stronger, calmer, less vulnerable then I really am. But that does not mean that the positive aspects of my character that other people see are mere illusions.

I would like to use a common everyday experience famil-iar to many of us to bring into clearer relief the difficulties that these two mutually exclusive answers to the question "Who am I?" can pose. As a mother, one is often forced by the nature of one's role to act stronger than one is. Mother, as we all know, always has things under control, but inside she may well be feeling totally miserable and exhausted. This division in the self, this need to be strong when feeling weak, to be courageous when feeling afraid, to provide the security one does not feel oneself, this division in the self can threaten our inner equilibrium. But I have learned from this poem of Bonhoeffer's to put up with this division and not to repress or exaggerate either of these experiences of self. The role in which I find myself is not an external thing alone; it is also a part of myself. Yet I still feel like a hypocrite, as Bonhoeffer says, if I simply play it with equanimity. "A hypocrite before others, and before myself a contemptibly woebegone weakling"—that is the accusation we throw at ourselves.

Who am I? Bonhoeffer does not make the answer easy for himself or for us. He does not just content himself with one of the two possibilities. The poem closes with a letting-go of the self, as it were; it closes with a prayer: "Whoever I am, thou knowest, O God, I am thine."

Is that nothing but a pious retreat, a flight from the question of who I am? We might think so, but I see in these closing words a strength and a step forward, a step into that darkness in which I cannot know anymore who I am. Dietrich Bonhoeffer accepts this ignorance about himself. There are situations in which our own identity becomes questionable, unclear, dishonest. In dark times like that, some people start drinking heavily or find some other way to treat themselves like throwaway objects. But Bonhoeffer prays: "O God, I am thine." The objective language gives way to a more personal tone; a "you" is addressed. I do not belong to myself. My identity is not a part of my consciousness. I do not know myself, and I "leave that all behind," as the mystics would say. I let all those things fall away: the images that others have of me and that could help me back onto my feet, the roles that prove me to be strong. I let those things go, but I let my image of myself go, too. I relinquish my own depression. I refuse the false comfort I could take from my friends' image of me, but I also do something more difficult still: I do not accept my depression as a final judgment over me. I go out of myself; I let myself go; I do not belong to myself; I do not hold my life in my own hands, especially not when I am in the dark night of self-condemnation, self-analysis, and depression.

It is a yielding up of the self, and the most difficult thing about it is to give up one's own sadness and leave that behind. And that is the point at which I begin to pray.

Who am I? I give this question back to him who was here before me. I give it back to the mystery of life. I have life on loan. It has been lent to me. It is not in my hands. There are situations in which I forget myself, forget my identity. I become nameless. But my name has been written in the book of life, even though it was not I who wrote it there.

In the biblical view, we have all—with Adam—eaten of the tree of knowledge. We know and want to know what good and evil are. But there is still another tree in God's garden, and that is the tree of life. We have not eaten of that tree. We have taken possession of knowledge but not of life itself. We do not really belong to ourselves. "I am yours" means that I do not set my hopes on the path of knowledge anymore. I am waiting for that other tree instead; I want to eat of that one.

Erich Fromm writes: "There is ... still another way that leads to comprehension of the human mystery. This is not the way of reflection but the way of love. Love is the active permeating and penetrating of another person whereby the desire for knowledge is satisfied by union. We have eaten of the tree of knowledge. We cannot simply eat of the tree of life. Only if we become one with God do we eat of it, do we truly share in life. In union I know you, I know myself, I know everyone—and I 'know' nothing. I learn in the only way that knowledge of life is possible for human beings—through union. The only thing that leads us to complete understanding is an act of love that goes beyond thought and words."

It is just such an act of love we find recorded at the end of this poem that Bonhoeffer wrote some months before his death. Words become superfluous. God is addressed; then the speaker is silent.

The poem "Someday" is by Sarah Kirsch:

Someday I will be unconscionably happy,
the news will come to me, I don't know
if we'll have summer or mushy snow, maybe
I'll be peeling potatoes (trying without
putting the knife down to make a single peel)

somebody will hear before I do, will tell me
on the phone, I may not answer,
I put the receiver down, smoke a cigarette,
turn the radio on, water the flowers
or go out onto the street into shops onto squares
and see that everything is the same as ever:
people push to get ahead in line, elsewhere
a demonstration is being organized, a microphone
    tested,
the speaker is writing a boring speech

on this day
I will love march music and shawms,
I am waiting for it, the day when the news reaches me
the war is over, those I do not call
my brothers, drop
a swarm of flies, with their airplanes, ships,
cannons
back into their country

This is a cheerful poem, one that makes us happy. The question "Who am I?" is answered in another dimension here, in the dimension of the future, of a utopia, a hope, a dream. The dream that is dreamt here is one of humankind's oldest dreams—the dream of peace.

"Someday I will be unconscionably happy." This formulation makes clear that I have been happy before but that I have not been able to be happy with good conscience. I have known about war and poverty. My personal happiness has been dampened by the pangs of conscience that an awareness of widespread misery brings. But someday things will be different. The news will come, breaking into my daily routine. At this point in the poem we still do not know what the news will be, but the happiness it brings is detailed here in the form of everyday activities, detailed slowly, epically, colloquially, humorously, and a bit ironically: peeling potatoes, telephoning, smoking, watering the flowers—peaceful occupations that are now possible without guilt, without complexes, without forgetting reality. In this routine day, the atmosphere of peace is already present. Then the news arrives: The war is over.

My acquaintance with this poem has been curious. When I first read it, I was in a state of increasing despair over the new phase the arms race had entered. I read that wonderful news, "The war is over," and I immediately thought of the medium-range missiles, the arms buildup that our government has chosen to camouflage under the term *Nachrüsten*.[*] Someday, I thought, there will be no more NATO. Someday Germany will be like Holland. The majority of our people—like the majority of the Dutch—will vote for peace and end our war, the economic one that we are conducting against the world's starving peoples. My taxes, I dreamed, will be used for irrigation projects and tractors that will help feed the poor. Sarah Kirsch is speaking here, I thought, about those who have the most and best planes, ships, artillery—speaking about us. The phrase "those I do not call my brothers" I read to mean those politicians whose Sunday speeches are always full of references to our brothers and sisters in the East Zone.

But in rereading the poem, I began to doubt this political interpretation. Sarah Kirsch, from whose volume *Landaufenthalt* (Country Sojourn) this poem comes, emigrated from East Germany to West Berlin in 1977. Is it—I thought

---

[*]TRANSLATORS' NOTE: *Nachrüsten* is a neologism suggesting that a potential enemy has gained a lead in the arms race and has thus forced one to undertake "retroarmament" to meet this threat.

all of a sudden—the Russians whom she does not call her brothers? Should this poem be read as a kind of literature of resistance? I then saw that the volume appeared in 1967 and realized that the poem must have been written somewhat earlier than that. The timing suggests that the author may have been thinking about Vietnam. How many poems after 1965 have the Vietnam War as their theme!

This political ambiguity of the text is one of the poem's virtues. It remains and will remain current, for the great dream of peace does not become superfluous with the end of just one or another war, hot or cold. There are still people whom—because of their planes, ships, and nuclear bombs—I do not want to call my brothers.

The important thing in terms of our main subject here is how the question "Who am I?" is answered. It is not answered solely in the dimension of individuality. My identity also includes my dreams and desires. The question "Who am I?" also asks who I want to be and what I hope for.

We learn most about other human beings, perhaps, when they reveal to us their innermost hopes and wishes and tell us how they conceive of happiness. It is important to learn that a description of happiness that depicts nothing but a sunny island for two people is wrong, superficial, inhuman. It is not enough to define identity in purely individual terms. Human beings whose dreams do not reach beyond those a mouse might have are underdeveloped human beings. As the American Indians would say, such persons have walked with only one of the four winds. They have parted company with the way of the eagle and the bear. They have cut themselves off from the wishes of humankind, from the hunger of the hungry. It is a dreadful sign of the psychic death prevalent in our country that the majority of our citizens have not made peace their theme, their wish, their prayer, their program for action. This psychic death becomes all the more horrendous if we compare our country with Holland, where there is a mass movement for peace and where people have learned from the experience of the Second World War. All we Germans have learned is forgetfulness and repression.

Perhaps some of you will be disturbed that I am not speaking softly and meditatively now but loudly and clearly. But I cannot divide myself into a religious and a political self. Religion and politics belong together for me. I understand the student who wants to go to Athos or Nicaragua, and I love Sarah Kirsch's poem because it tells us so much about happiness. I would not dare to speak of Bonhoeffer's mysticism if I were not trying to live in the tradition of his struggle.

I cannot divide myself in two any more than Sarah Kirsch can. The personal *is* the political. Even potato peeling will become an art once the war is over. We are waiting for a new heaven and a new earth, and our identity is located in a place where we have never yet been, in humanity's true home, a world without war. "O God, I am thine" means that I can yield myself up, but it also means that my life's wishes do not have to be small and fearful. They can be as grand as the wishes and promises of him to whom I belong. God's wish for us is that we—in our outward lives and in our deepest and fondest dreams—become instruments of peace. His promise to us is that we will rid ourselves of everything that stands in the way of his kingdom, that we will make cruise missiles into school buses.

We began these reflections on "Who am I?" with a children's song. If we asked children to consider this question and talked with them about it, we would probably find that many of them would begin their answers the way Sarah Kirsch began her poem: "Someday. . . ." I hope so, and I will close with the wish that all of us will never become so grown up that we no longer begin by saying "Someday . . ." if someone asks who we are.

References

In this volume reference is made to the following books and periodicals, which are listed in the order of their use.

K.-W. Bühler, *Der Warenhimmel auf Erden. Triviale Religion im Konsumzeitalter* (Wuppertal, 1973).

G. Bormann, *Theorie und Praxis kirchlicher Organisation. Ein Beitrag zum Problem der Rückständigkeit sozialer Gruppen* (Cologne, 1969).

Dorothee Soelle, *Christ the Representative: An Essay in Theology After the Death of God* (Fortress Press, 1967).

———, *Death by Bread Alone: Texts and Reflections on Religious Experience* (Fortress Press, 1978).

———, *Beyond Mere Obedience* (Pilgrim Press, 1982).

Dietrich Bonhoeffer, *Letters and Papers from Prison*, enlarged edition, edited by Eberhard Bethge (Macmillan Co., 1977), pp. 347f.

Erich Fromm, *The Dogma of Christ, and Other Essays on Religion, Psychology and Culture* (Holt, Rinehart & Winston, 1963).

Sarah Kirsch, *Landaufenthalt* (Berlin and Weimar, 1967).